Painkillers and Gummi Bears

A mother and son's journey
through fear to freedom

Gail Stewart Frare
and
Christopher Thomas Stewart

ISBN: 1502997320
ISBN 13: 9781502997326
Library of Congress Control Number: 2014919458
CreateSpace Independent Publishing Platform
North Charleston, South Carolina

Dedication

This book is dedicated to my son and co-author, Christopher. Writing this book has brought you alive again in so many ways.

This book is also dedicated to our family--the good people we were before, and the more authentic people we have become.

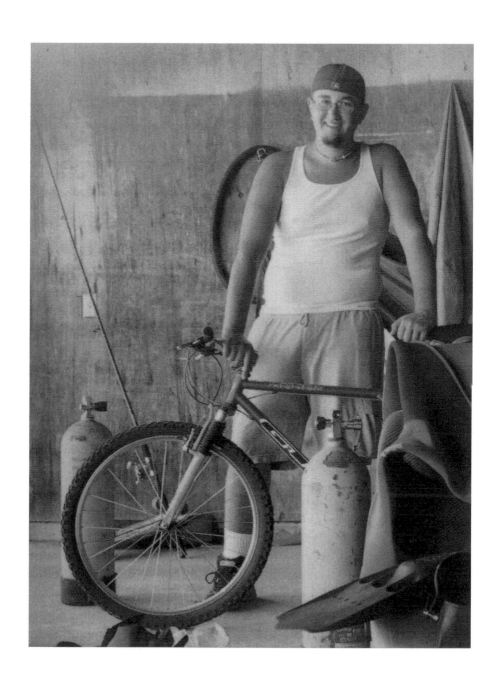

Lucky

Christopher Thomas Stewart, age seventeen

Supposedly I am lucky
say those who humbly assume to know it all.
Lucky that I have had a second chance.
I disagree.

I ask you, the "expert,"
please tell me,
how can a youth stolen by a diseased heart be a gift?
Never mind the details escape you.

All you wish to see are appearances.
What lies beneath rocks your boat,
so you exercise selective eyes.

It is comforting to perceive that the healing is complete—
that the zipper scar on my chest is the only wound.
Your assumptions are much easier than touching the truth.
That rotten fruit lies beyond
your lip service attempts at understanding.

What? You know how I feel?
You know the smells of the ICU
with tubes like vines into veins to strangle?
Or the knowledge that someone had to die so you may live?

So I'm sorry if I don't care
about your girlfriend leaving you.
I am jaded to standard problems.
My apologies for being hardened.
I have a stranger's heart in my chest.
A heart that, with every beat, reminds me my time is borrowed
and that I never wished to be a miracle.

Prologue

Few would call my son Christopher lucky, as the poem suggests. A heart transplant at fifteen stole his youth, and he was dead from cancer at twenty-two. This is his story.

The idea for this book came from Christopher, and it was to be his to write. Christopher Thomas Stewart had plans to write *Painkillers and Gummi Bears*—an apt title describing the loss of his childhood innocence due to a random illness. The idea of writing a book came to him as he was preparing for a stem cell transplant. That transplant was a last-ditch effort to save him from an aggressive cancer. The book was his way of looking death in the face with some hope of survival while achieving the third-party objectivity of a reporter as he recorded his thoughts and the events of each day.

He did not survive to write that book. My husband purchased a digital recorder for him, and he set out recording his activities, thoughts, and emotions with the thoroughness and zeal of any good journalist. As March 2003 turned into April and then May, his recordings diminished, and he asked me to record updates for him every few days. The recorder ended up under a pile of get well soon cards. Christopher succumbed to his cancer on June 13, 2004, at the age of almost twenty-three.

Ten years after his death, newly found journal entries from his freshman year in college ignited my passion to write *Painkillers and Gummi Bears* for Christopher. It was as if my son nudged me from the grave. "What about that book, Mom?" I include him as an author since he wrote so many of the passages and even chapters in this book. His words throughout are in a bolder font.

"True, unadulterated joy in my life is to write at least one piece of literary mastery," Christopher wrote. *"I don't care if it is [discovered] after I'm dead because that is how all famous writers do it."*

Christopher was a study in emotional extremes. He felt deeply, and his feelings ranged from crippling anxiety and melancholy to intense joy and love of life. His high school group of ragtag friends knew he loved them fiercely. I also knew that deep love and bonded to him like no other human being. When he was little, I had empathy for the sweet egg-headed goofball of a boy. I had also pushed back against anxiety most of my life. We both knew that fear—baseless, faceless, and nameless. I wanted to protect Christopher from those fears. He loved and needed me in a way my older son and husband did not.

I was a registered nurse with a cardiac specialty. My anxiety had always tilted me toward hypochondria and worries about my children's health. I worried about crippling heart conditions because I knew so much about them. As my sons grew, though, I finally became confident they had no more chance of contracting some crazy, rare disease than anyone else. After all, viral cardiomyopathy occurred in only six of one hundred thousand people. I relaxed.

At age fifteen, post-viral cardiomyopathy spiraled Christopher into near fatal heart failure. He required a heart transplant. Six years later, the antirejection medications he required so his body would not reject the heart depleted his immune system. They left him wide open to an aggressive form of cancer.

Surprisingly when the real reasons for fear came, Christopher and I found our footing. Through seven years of medical hell, we broke through the fear prisons that had trapped and limited us, and we faced some of the most difficult circumstances possible. Christopher and I (the "weak ones") carried the strong ones on our shoulders. While I became the clearheaded nurse-mom able to care for Christopher until his death, Christopher comforted his family and friends in the end.

First suffering breaks you, then it strengthens you. When things were most grim, a deepening occurred, and unimaginable serenity and glimpses of joy emerged. That strength was a gift from Christopher's illness, and it has allowed me to live my life in an entirely new way.

Christopher's poem "Lucky" was written when he was still angry and working through his newly created "normal" after the heart transplant. The seven years from heart transplant to cancer were not all challenging. After the initial eighteen months of recovery, Christopher actually had some very good and happy years. He had a zeal for international politics as a student at The Evergreen State College and was working through his junior year of college when the cancer struck. He was dead twelve months later.

This story is Christopher's but also mine. I cannot separate the two. We were inextricably linked in life and now also in his death. With his words and my own, I tell our story. Its trajectory is decidedly dark, but small and then large blessings seeped through the cracks of despair. These events changed our lives in subtly positive ways not previously imagined. To say we were lucky might be a stretch, but peace and fearlessness are gifts beyond compare. We would not have received those gifts if our lives had not been ripped apart.

I tell *Painkillers and Gummi Bears* with Christopher's title and our shared words. I do so with the wish that those suffering losses will take hope that the experiences will not be irreparably crushing but transformative.

Chapter 1

Free Fall

The words "seared into memory" made complete sense after Monday, April 7, 1997. The phone call came in from Eastern Washington. I knew my son Christopher had not been feeling well. In fact, he had had some alarming symptoms.

"I have to take this call," I told my coworkers.

I was in a meeting that morning at Providence Centralia Hospital, my workplace. I walked into the administrative suite and asked to use a phone.

"Use Mitzi's office," said Shannon, referring to our nurse executive.

I hurried into Mitzi's office and dialed the phone.

"Pullman Memorial Hospital," the voice said on the line.

I knew Christopher was going there that morning, so I explained who I was. I was directed to the emergency room and connected to the Emergency Room physician.

"Mrs. Stewart? I am Doctor Worden here in the emergency room at Pullman Memorial Hospital at Washington State University, and I am with your two wonderful sons. I have examined Christopher, and your boys tell me you are a nurse. I can go over the specifics of what I have found with you, but it is not good news. Your son Christopher's heart is about the size of a football. He is in very serious heart failure."

My own heart started racing, and my mind spun as the doctor continued to talk.

"We did a chest X-ray because of Christopher's shortness of breath. When I first saw it, I thought he must have a large fluid collection around his heart, so I ordered an ultrasound. There was no fluid around his heart, though. Your son's heart has dilated terribly and is working poorly. He needs immediate attention at a major medical center. I am so sorry. I have two boys about the same age, and they are good friends like your sons. I am taking extra special care of your boys for you."

"Thank you so much," I said, but my mind was racing. Christopher was on the far eastern side of Washington State. We lived in Olympia, Washington, on the west side of the state. How were we going to get him home? My mind was reeling, trying to think what to do next.

"I presume you want him airlifted back over to Western Washington," Dr. Worden said.

A nurse by training, I started my career in a coronary care unit. Later I organized a cardiac rehabilitation program. I knew when a heart was the size of a football and the word "airlift" was mentioned, things were very serious.

The previous Friday fifteen-year-old Christopher had flown to Washington State University (WSU) in Pullman for spring break with his brother. His big brother, Jeff, was a freshman at WSU. I am not sure why the boys' father, Tom, and I thought this was a wise idea, but at the time it seemed exciting for Christopher to go visit his brother at college. A few days before he left, Christopher was complaining about some lower right-sided chest pain, but I thought it was a muscle strain from his weight lifting. He was doing weights as part of his fitness regimen for football. I found out later the day he boarded the plane, Friday, April 4, he was not feeling very well, but he didn't want me to know because he didn't want his trip canceled.

Once he was in Pullman with his brother, we talked every day.

"Hey!" I heard as I picked up the phone Saturday evening. That was Christopher's way of saying hello.

"Hey to you," I said. "How's your trip going?"

"Pretty good," Christopher said. "I think I ate some bad hamburger at a barbecue this afternoon, though. My stomach is really upset, and I feel like I am going to hurl."

College freshmen having a barbecue and getting food poisoning didn't seem out of the realm of possibility, so I let it go. "How is the pain in your side, honey?" I asked.

"Man, it is still giving me grief," he said. "I must have pulled something lifting weights."

"Are you taking Tylenol or anything for it?"

"No."

"OK. Get your brother to take you to the store, and get some Tylenol and ibuprofen. Take it as directed. If this is a pulled muscle, that will make it feel much better." I was both a mom and a nurse. I knew some beer might well be involved but didn't ask. I preferred not to know. "Remember to get and take that medicine, and call me tomorrow night to check in, OK? Remember, we are trusting you to be good."

"I know, Mom," Christopher said with a bit of disgust in his voice. "I'll call you tomorrow night. Love you. Bye."

I thought about the pain in Christopher's side. I knew the only things in that area of the body were the liver and gallbladder—not likely to be problems at his age. It had to be a pulled muscle or some strained cartilage.

That evening Jeff called. "Mom, Christopher doesn't look good. He is still very sick to his stomach and can't keep anything down. His breathing is also kind of weird when he's sleeping. We haven't done much today because he hasn't felt good."

I asked to talk to Christopher.

"Hey," he said in sort of a grunt.

"Still not feeling good from that bad burger?"

"Guess so. The pain is killing me," he said. Something was not adding up here, and all the nurse hairs on the back of my neck started standing up when Christopher said, "The pain is making it hard to breathe."

At that point Jeff promised to take Christopher to the campus hospital in the morning. My husband, Tom, was doing his usual, "I am sure he will be fine" routine. He often thought I was overreacting, and he was usually right. Most things turned out OK. Nonetheless I had trouble going to sleep that night after worrying about my youngest son.

Monday morning I got to work and called Jeff's dorm room. There was no answer. *Good*, I thought. *They did what I asked and went right to the hospital.* When I hadn't received a call by 9:00 a.m., I called again and got Christopher on the phone. "Christopher, I worried all night. Have you already been to the hospital?"

"No. And I feel like stool," he said with his normal uncouthness.

"Sweetheart, I think this is serious, and I am really worried. You need to tell Jeff to get his ass out of bed and get you to a doctor *now*."

By the time they got to the hospital, Jeff was starting to freak out. He loved his brother but had always thought of him as a wuss. He had been merciless about Christopher being sick. At the barbecue he had made Christopher get up and run for Frisbees. "Get off your ass, lead butt," Jeff had said. (This was one of his favorite expressions with his brother.) Today, though, Christopher's shortness of breath, poor color, and weakness frightened them as they walked the short distance to the campus hospital. He barely made it. Then came the call from Dr. Worden.

Heart failure. Major medical center. Airlift. I could barely think straight, but I heard myself telling Dr. Worden that my sister, Chris, worked closely with Airlift Northwest. Would it work to contact them? They could take Christopher to Harborview Medical Center in Seattle, and then we would decide if he should stay there or where he should go. Airlift Northwest was the medical air ambulance service for Western Washington and Alaska.

"That would work fine," Dr. Worden said. "I can get the contact information here and will call back to confirm when all the arrangements are made."

Hallelujah and thank you, God! I can't remember who called my sister—the doctor or me—but within minutes arrangements had been made, and a Learjet was dispatched to Pullman to pick up my son and return him to Seattle. It was not special treatment to be air transported, but it was so comforting to know my sister, Chris, an RN, was involved and would get Christopher safely to where he needed to be.

Almost ten years later, I can still picture myself sitting at that phone and talking to the doctor as if I was someone observing from the other side of the room. Time sped up and slowed down all at once. My fingers and brain fumbled as I tried to remember phone numbers and how to dial. I called Tom.

"Hilger-Stewart Construction," the receptionist said.

"Sandy, this is Gail. Is Tom in the office?" *Please say yes!* my panicky mind was saying.

"Yes. He's here," she said. "Hang on a minute."

"Tom Stewart," Tom said.

"Hey. It's me," I said, and I immediately teared up at the sound of his voice.

"Did you hear from the boys? How is Christopher?" he asked.

"He is very sick," I said. I was fighting back tears and trying not to sound as hysterical as I felt. "You aren't going to believe this, but he's in very bad heart failure." My brain was screaming at me as I spoke to Tom. How could I miss something like that? How could my fifteen-year-old son be in heart failure?

There was silence on the other end of the phone for a moment as he took this in. "OK. What's the plan?" Tom said in his tight-lipped, quiet, and super-controlled manner.

"They are flying him to Harborview in Seattle. You and I need to get there as soon as possible," I said. "Tom, this could be deadly serious. This could mean a heart transplant."

Tom usually minimized everything I said when it came to health matters. As both a hypochondriac and a nurse, I almost always thought the worst. This time, however, Tom could tell there was no added melodrama.

"We will handle whatever it is," he said in a clipped voice. "I will meet you at home as soon as I can get there, and we'll head to Seattle."

"OK," I replied and hung up the phone.

I returned to my meeting with tears in my eyes and a blotchy red face. Soon I was heading home to meet Tom. I must have driven ninety miles per hour. It was a gorgeous spring day, and as I whizzed by blossoming cherry trees and green grass, all I could think about was why everything looked so normal when my son's life had just spun totally out of control.

Christopher was diagnosed with post-viral idiopathic dilated cardiomyopathy. This mouthful describes the heart damage some experience after a viral illness. It is not any specific virus—just a viral illness usually six weeks or so before the heart damage is found. "Idiopathic" meant the doctors didn't know exactly what caused it. "Cardiomyopathy" meant the heart muscle was severely damaged, the chambers dilated, and the muscle walls thinned. Heart function was greatly reduced. We were all going to find out very soon that the number one symptom for young people with Christopher's new and unwelcome condition was sudden death. Thank God sudden death in Pullman was not how Christopher was diagnosed.

Tom and I drove from Olympia sixty miles north to Seattle and into the emergency entrance of Harborview Medical Center. We got there just as the ambulance arrived from Boeing Field carrying Christopher and Jeff. Jeff was the first one out of the ambulance, and my initial thought was that *he* looked terrible. To say he was as white as a sheet was an understatement.

"Sweetheart," I said, and I rushed to him and gave him a big hug. "You don't look too good. Are you OK?"

He hugged me tightly. Jeff later admitted he was scared to death he was at fault for nearly killing his brother. He had let Christopher have a heyday with unlimited beer and salty junk food the night he arrived.

"God, Mom, it was awful," Jeff said. "He got so blue and out of breath walking the short distance to the hospital, and when they told us what was wrong, I about passed out. I made Christopher go to breakfast with me before we went to the hospital. What an idiot I am! I am so sorry." Jeff was clearly feeling guilty. He brightened a little as he said, "Christopher does feel better now since he has peed a ton."

We hugged Christopher on the gurney as they wheeled him into the emergency room.

"What the hell happened to you?" Tom said as he ruffled his hair.

Christopher replied, "Man, I have felt really rough the last few days. Right now I can breathe better. I have been peeing like a racehorse since they gave me some medicine to get fluid out of my system."

They had given him a big dose of a medication called Lasix. This allowed him to turn much of the excess fluid taxing his heart into urine and get rid of it.

"God, I could hardly get to that hospital," Christopher said with tears flowing down his cheeks. "I felt as if I had weights in my legs, and I was breathing like a chimney. It scared the crap out of me."

He wiped away the tears with the back of his hand. He was only fifteen—still a little boy in some ways. I was so glad to have him in my sight and in the care of this emergency room where my sister was the nursing director.

The medical director of the emergency department came to examine Christopher. A man of few words, he did a quick examination and said some tests would be ordered. "Do you know where you want Christopher to be hospitalized—UW or Children's?"

The medical director was referring to University of Washington Medical Center (UWMC) and Children's Orthopedic Hospital (COH). Both were in Seattle. By age he would go to Children's, but he was also 6'2" and over two hundred pounds.

"Both are willing to take Chris," the doctor said. "Of course, the social worker at COH insists he is a pediatric patient and should come to them."

"Where do you think he should go?" I asked.

The doctor crossed his arms and thought a minute. "Given Christopher's size, I think UWMC would be the best choice. The fact he is at UWMC doesn't preclude someone from COH coming over to do a pediatric cardiology consult. Chris, is that OK with you?"

Christopher shrugged his shoulders. "I'm hardly a baby. I don't want to go to a pediatric hospital. UWMC sounds fine with me."

Arrangements were made. Jeff headed to my sister's house in Seattle to get some sleep and join us later. Christopher was admitted to the hospital, and continuous heart monitoring began. Soon after he was admitted, the head of the Heart Failure Service, Dr. Daniel Fishbein, came to see him.

When we first arrived in Seattle, we all felt energized from adrenaline, being together, and knowing Christopher would receive good care.

Now that was beginning to fade. Christopher was uncomfortable, still had significant pain in his right side, and was very restless in the bed. Food didn't sound good to him, and the fact something was extremely wrong with him was starting to penetrate.

Dr. Fishbein examined Christopher in the evening. Dr. Fishbein was of average height, had short brown hair that was balding on top, and wore black glasses and a crisp baby blue shirt with the sleeves rolled up. From the moment he spoke, it was clear from his accent he was from the East Coast. He walked over to us and extended his hand. "Hello. I am Daniel Fishbein." We both shook his hand and thanked him for coming. He looked at the chart. "Do you like to be called Christopher or Chris?" Dr. Fishbein asked.

"Everybody but my mom and dad call me Chris," our son said and shook Dr. Fishbein's hand.

"OK," Dr. Fishbein said. "Tell me, Chris, what is going on. What led up to you being here today?"

Christopher told the tale of feeling badly but going to visit his brother anyway and everything else that had happened since.

Using the stethoscope Dr. Fishbein listened carefully to Christopher's chest. "You have fluid in your lungs. It has accumulated because your heart isn't working right. That's why it's hard to breathe when you are lying flat. The medicine started today will continue to get rid of that fluid and make you more comfortable.

"Thinking back over the past several weeks, have you been sick at all? Did you by chance have a viral illness or something like that?" Dr. Fishbein asked, and he continued his exam.

Christopher looked at me. "Mom, when did you and Dad go skiing and Grandma took care of me?"

Right! I thought. *The ski trip when we made Christopher stay home.* He'd had a fever and felt lousy, and we left him with my mother in Olympia. He'd gone to a paintball party when he was not yet fully recovered.

"That was February nineteenth to twenty-fourth," Tom said.

Dr. Fishbein jotted down a few notes. "So that was about six weeks ago."

As a cardiac nurse, I had a premonition. The diagnosis we were soon to hear came slamming into my brain. I started shaking, and my gut clenched. I tried to breathe calmly so I didn't make a scene.

"Did you eat a lot of salty food at WSU?" Dr. Fishbein asked.

"I guess so," Chris said. "Chips and burgers. Stuff like that."

"Maybe a bit of beer?" Dr. Fishbein said with a smile.

Christopher turned red and hung his head. "Well, yeah. There were parties everywhere."

I was starting to get the picture. Beer and salty food had created the perfect storm for Christopher's silent heart problem to blow up like a volcano.

"Chris, we need to get that fluid off your system. The severe pain in your right side is from fluid pressure on your liver. And most importantly we need to do some tests to try to determine why your heart is not working properly."

In retrospect I believe the doctor purposely didn't use the term "heart failure." For that I am glad. Christopher later came to hate that term.

For several days I could not remember the doctor's name. I knew it was Dr. Fishstein or Dr. Fish something. The memory was gone. I had been too stressed. Tom and I stayed in the room with Christopher for what turned into an eight-day hospital stay.

The first few nights, we got no sleep. Christopher's oxygen-starved body caused him to be constantly moving and restless. A normal resting heart rate is sixty to one hundred beats per minute. Christopher's resting heart rate hovered around 120, even with oxygen constantly administered. That rate increased substantially with any activity or emotion. When a heart is enlarged and in distress, it causes the upper chest to "heave." We could see Christopher's every heartbeat through his hospital gown. He couldn't lie flat, and he coughed incessantly the first few nights.

While Christopher tried to sleep, I lay there with what-ifs going through my mind. I was searching my brain for the previous weeks. How had I missed this? The trip to visit Jeff, all that salty food, the paintball party when he was barely recovering from his virus that included a sore throat and a fever of 102 degrees for three to four days. Paintball parties, I knew, consisted of going into the forest in camouflage gear, running around like crazy people with paintball guns, and playing army. Had that extreme activity while ill caused this? My self-critical mind was having a heyday, and I was making myself sick with guilt.

All week Christopher had tests. The echocardiogram test will forever haunt me. Christopher had to lie flat for over an hour, and he felt as if he was drowning. He had to stop the test a number of times to catch his breath. The initially talkative and jovial technician became increasingly quiet as the exam proceeded. We could tell she did not like what she saw.

Dr. Fishbein saw Christopher daily. On the evening of the third day, after all the tests had been run, he came in and sat in a chair beside the bed. "Chris, what I think you have has a big long scary name—post-viral dilated cardiomyopathy. The febrile illness you had six weeks ago damaged your heart. It caused it to dilate and go into what is called heart failure. There is no immediate 'fix' to this disease. Instead the goal is to support the heart, reduce the strain on it as much as possible, and hope it will heal over time.

"Your echocardiogram was very telling. That test measures the ejection fraction—the percentage of blood ejected from the heart with each heartbeat. A normal ejection fraction is sixty percent or better. Christopher, yours is at eight percent. That is an indication of the severest form of heart failure—what we call stage four."

We heard the doctor's words. We even knew what they meant. Yet we were all in shock. Christopher sat in his bed, and tears started to run down his cheeks. Soon we were all crying.

Dr. Fishbein went on. "The statistics are that six people out of every one hundred thousand will get a dilated cardiomyopathy, so it is rare. Of those, twenty percent will get completely well, sixty percent will get better but will need ongoing medication, and twenty percent will get worse and might need heart transplantation." He hurried on. "I have no idea at this time where you fall on this healing continuum."

The tears turned to downright sobs all around. Tom and I held on to Christopher.

"I am so sorry to give you this news," Dr. Fishbein said. "There are medications we will start you on, but they have to be carefully titrated to be sure you can tolerate them. You will be here several days until we get you on the best regimen. Then you will go home, and it will be a bit of a waiting game to see how much your heart improves."

After the doctor left the room, the sobbing continued for a long time. Christopher held on to me for dear life. He was crying, angry, and panicked. "God, Mom, why me? Why is this happening to me?" he wailed.

"Honey, I have no idea."

"Christopher," said Tom, "we are going to beat this. We are a strong family, and we are with you one hundred percent. You are going to land on your feet."

The nurse came in several times looking concerned. All this emotion had triggered adrenaline, and Christopher's heart rate was dangerously high. He was having many irregular heartbeats. They finally gave him some Ativan to calm him, and he finally settled down and slept.

Tom and I clung to each other. We didn't talk. There was nothing to say. We held each other as the waves of grief swallowed us up.

There was another week in the hospital while Christopher's medications were adjusted. His appetite started to return. He began taking short walks around the hospital ward. Jeff came back from college for a visit.

"I can't concentrate knowing what is going on here with Christopher," he said. "I am glad for your calls every day, but it is hard to not be here with you. I have no idea what my grades are going to be. Right now I am just aiming to pass."

Jeff hit Christopher softly in the arm. "How are you doing? Really?" he said to his brother.

Christopher had shrunken over the week. Some of it was the fluid loss, but he also had hardly eaten anything. He looked wan and pale. "I have lost trust in my body. I am a young kid who should be hanging out with my friends and doing stupid stuff. I can't believe I'm here in this fucking nightmare. That's how I am," he said and wiped tears away angrily with the back of his hand.

Jeff had nothing to say to this. He just hung his head and nodded.

Christopher was so angry with the diagnosis of heart failure. "'Heart failure.' That is the *stupidest* name! If my heart failed, I'd be dead. I hate that name. It's just stupid."

It was such a scary term, and to think his heart was failing was an unbelievably awful and claustrophobic feeling. He couldn't run away from it, ignore it, or make it go away.

By day seven Christopher's medications were where Dr. Fishbein wanted them. A series of blood and skin tests had been done to screen Christopher in the unlikely event he would ever need a new heart. The nurse in me had a feeling this was not a routine test, and he might well need a transplant. On this day's visit, Dr. Fishbein explained Christopher's meds to him.

"Chris," he said, "there is a type of medication taken for heart failure that we have to titrate very carefully. It's called enalapril, and this is the one we have been slowly increasing each day. It has been shown to be very helpful to patients in heart failure. It decreases the workload of the heart. If you get too much, your blood pressure gets too low, and it can worsen your heart function. Since day three we have been increasing your dose by two and a half milligrams per day and watching your blood pressure closely. You are now on the optimal dose.

"I know you will hate this last medicine, Coumadin. It is a blood-thinning agent, and with it you need blood tests twice a week to be sure your level is safe. It is a hard drug to regulate, but you need it to prevent any blood clots from forming in your heart. If that happened and the blood clot broke off and floated downstream, it would either lodge in your lung or brain. Either circumstance would most probably be fatal."

I hated the thought of my fifteen-year-old son on Coumadin. That was an old person's medication, goddamnit. I kept these thoughts to myself. I could not stop thinking about how I could have missed this. I was a nurse for God's sake. I worked in a coronary care unit. I started a cardiac rehabilitation program, but I had missed this. Then I asked why. Why my son? This was my question to God for a long, long time.

Chapter 2

Heart Failure? I'm Fifteen Years Old!

Christopher was discharged on April 15 with a medication list that would have looked normal for an eighty-five-year-old. It was heartbreaking for him and me, a nurse and mom of a fifteen-year-old. We were to follow up with a local cardiologist in Olympia and have regular appointments at the University Hospital's heart failure clinic. He was to eat a very low-salt diet, engage in very little activity, and have lots of blood pressure monitoring, especially before each medication dose.

Christopher felt quite washed-out the day of discharge, and it took all day for them to release us. We wanted out of there so badly. It was an agonizing wait from early morning when the doctor told us we could go home until we finally had the discharge instructions late in the day.

My son was euphoric about getting out of the hospital. After a night's sleep in his own bed, he felt much better the next day. He was sitting in his favorite chair—the big denim love seat in the family room. His old smile came back, and he wanted to eat. He was *starved*.

The biggest joy killer to Christopher was the salt restriction. Table salt (sodium) had to be severely restricted. Sodium causes the body to retain fluid, and his heart could not pump any extra fluid.

When Christopher was a toddler and my little buddy going to town and running errands, we would frequently break up our days by going to those delightful little restaurants with play areas—later known as fast food. Before all that came to be known as addictive, high-fat, and high-salt food, Christopher associated this food and setting as wonderful times with Mom.

"Let's run by Burger King today, Mom," he would say in his little three-year-old voice.

I indulged and came to regret this for the rest of my days.

Christopher *loved* fast food. No matter what I tried, there were too many times we hurriedly got pizza, hamburgers, or burritos—everything with tons of salt. To take salt out of Christopher's food was to make it totally unpalatable to him. This became a huge quality of life issue for him. He had hardly eaten a thing off the hospital menu and had little appetite until he got home eight days later.

I had an American Heart Association cookbook they had given me with many recipes for from-scratch foods Christopher could eat. He decided what he wanted to try, and I went to the store and bought all the ingredients. For the next few days, I spent hours preparing recipes Christopher would try and immediately reject as tasteless. He was starving, and everything I cooked tasted terrible to him. He was dying for salt and started sneaking tortilla chips. I cannot explain how scared, hopeless, and exhausted I felt trying to make this food that was admittedly tasteless. (I thought it tasted bad too!) We had tried to limit the amount of fat in our diets but never salt. This eating style was creating a nightmare now.

What kind of a mother are you? Why did you let your son have such a lousy diet that he won't eat healthy food now? The voices in my head were relentless with everything I had done wrong in the mothering department for the past fifteen years. This further burdened and exhausted me. I was hardly sleeping at night. I was on high alert for Christopher's breathing and his every action. I was so afraid he would collapse at home, and I would have to start CPR and get help. I was terrified my son was going to die.

The first weekend we were home, we had friends come stay from Canada. Why we thought that would work, I have no idea. It was horrible. I would frantically run around trying to play hostess, nurse, and healthy food cook, and I wouldn't let them help. They were miserable, and so was I. The only time I could relax for even a short while was in the evening when I would allow myself a glass of wine. That turned into a blessed relief from worry and something I cherished and looked forward to.

The second Saturday we were home was opening day of trout-fishing season. My husband's family had a cabin at a small lake outside Shelton, Washington, west of us. It was an annual Stewart family tradition to go fishing on opening weekend every year, and our boys had done this since they were barely old enough to hold fishing poles. Christopher was adamant we go. The nurse at the heart failure clinic thought it too far away from emergency care and advised us not to. Christopher was not feeling well and had very little energy. I was concerned, but Tom and I decided we were going to make this happen anyway. It felt to Christopher like a piece of normalcy, and we so wanted him to feel normal.

We put a small boat and a small electric trolling motor in the back of our pickup, and we headed west to the lake very early Saturday morning. Christopher slept all the way up for the hour drive. It was cold, and Christopher was chilled but determined to fish. He was a good angler and always caught his limit. It was a stocked lake, so chances for success were good. With Tom in the back of the boat, me in the front, and our son in the middle, we went fishing for an hour or two. I can still feel my heart breaking as I watched this young man try to recapture the joy of this experience in his debilitated state. Trout fishing is not a physically taxing activity, but after about an hour, Christopher was exhausted and freezing. We had to help him out of the boat, up the dock, and into his grandparents' cabin. We laid him down and covered him with lots of blankets. The cabin was very cold, so we built a fire in the woodstove and got it warm. We took several pictures that day, including one of Christopher with deep dark circles under his eyes sleeping in the cabin. I was so happy once we got home. I had feared the worst, and my adrenaline had been pumping all day. I felt I aged ten years in this one day.

I was starting to worry about certain things as I observed Christopher, and I compiled a list of questions to take to our follow-up visit with Dr. Fishbein on May 1st. Christopher's breathing during sleep was very erratic. Sometimes he would hardly breathe for twenty to thirty seconds, and then his chest would heave, and he would breathe as if he had just been running. This is called Cheyne-Stokes breathing, and I had seen this in very old, dying patients. Why the hell was my son doing this? Why did his breathing seem particularly bad when he took the anti-nausea medicine Compazine? After taking this medication Christopher fell asleep and then woke after a particularly long apneic spell. He felt as if he was dying. Later we found out this medicine can make end-stage heart failure much worse. As we had been told earlier, Christopher's ejection fraction was only 8 percent. This medication did almost kill him. A physician less expert in heart failure from Olympia had prescribed it, so I didn't blame him for not knowing.

Christopher ended up in the local emergency room, the hospital for three days, and the doctor's office twice over the next two weeks. The first visit to the cardiologist's office was after he went with his Grandpa Larry to a golf tournament. They rented a golf cart and had a great day. They also ate big fat salty Polish hot dogs. Christopher loved it, but it caused so much fluid weight gain that his right side was again painful. He ended up in the hospital a few days later with fifteen pounds of fluid built up in his abdomen and around his intestines.

I sensed the cardiologists at St. Peter in Olympia were uncomfortable treating Christopher because he was a child and his heart failure was so severe. While he was in the hospital, one of them prescribed a medication that caused a heart rhythm that could easily have been fatal if sustained. They immediately stopped this drug, but this left them with few drugs in their arsenal. The cardiologist who examined Christopher in the emergency department said before he admitted him, "We need to get him to Seattle so the big boys at the university can work a miracle. He is a very sick young man, and we don't have what is needed in our bag of tricks here."

I couldn't understand why Christopher wasn't transferred to University Hospital, but I did know the Olympia cardiologists were consulting with the heart failure specialists at the UW regularly. I should have pitched an absolute fit and demanded he be transferred to the University of Washington. I had always been a rule follower and never wanted to make waves. Like many nurses I found physicians somewhat intimidating, and I was following all the medical advice given for my son. I now wish I had thrown him in my car, driven the sixty miles to Seattle, shown up in the emergency room, and refused to leave until my son had the proper care. I worked in a very good hospital, but children as sick as Christopher were usually attended to at highly specialized medical centers where heart transplants were performed. The nurses at St. Peter were scared stiff taking care of him, and I totally understood. I didn't know whether I was more scared having him home or in this hospital, but either way I felt we were totally alone.

The three days Christopher was in the Olympia hospital were anxiety-ridden. This hospital was my place of employment, and due to the type of jobs I'd held, I knew literally everyone who worked there. I would run into physicians and hospital staff I knew, and they would ask me why I was there in street clothes. When I replied, "My youngest son, Christopher, was diagnosed with post-viral cardiomyopathy," I could see the instant recognition of the seriousness and randomness of this condition. It was as if the roulette wheel had spun, and my child was the unlucky one. Everyone was sympathetic, and there were many hugs and tears.

The second day of this hospitalization, Christopher looked ghastly. His color was a yellowish, bloodless pallor that almost matched the yellowish tan shirt he was wearing. One of my best nursing friends came by during her shift. She tried hard to mask her reaction when she saw him, but I saw it, and it confirmed the panic in my gut. *He is going to die!* my mind kept screaming. She later told me this was exactly what she felt also.

Tom went home to sleep and I stayed. That night in the hospital I couldn't sleep. By about 4:00 a.m., I was silently weeping and so distraught. I had always had a firm belief in God, but that night I felt totally alone, and I doubted there was a God. Having had a lifelong faith, to feel as if there was no benevolent force in the universe was the scariest notion of them all. It was as if my world was spinning out of control, and there was nothing I could hold onto. I was balled up in the fetal position on a horrible, uncomfortable cot that squeaked every time I moved. I was at the end of my ability to cope and was just shaking. I asked God for a sign he was really there and had us in his sight. I then fell asleep for a few hours.

At shift change a lovely nurse named Janice came into the room. She was so kind to Christopher and me. She told me she had been praying for us, and she had a sense of peace about her and a confidence others had not shown. She was a very calming presence at a time it was badly needed. A short time later, another great friend, Daidre, came to visit. Daidre and her husband had two boys almost identical in age to my sons. Daidre had lost her third son, Gabriel, to sudden infant death syndrome (SIDS) when he was five months old. It was a trauma and sorrow we had shared as young mothers many years before. I confided in Daidre how scared I was and that I didn't even know if there was a God. She held me, she cried with me, and she reassured me there was a God. She said he was there with us, and he would get us through this. All at once it dawned on me that these two women showing up in the early hours of the morning were signs from God that Christopher and I were not forgotten. There was some peace and awe with that realization.

Christopher went home on the third day, and we had only a few days to wait for the clinic appointment at the university. I could hardly wait to get him up to Seattle. If we could only keep him from dying before we got there! I was terrified those last two days. By this time Christopher was gravely ill. As I learned later, my intuition and clinical assessment were correct. He was near death. He couldn't keep down any food, and the only thing that sounded good to him was frozen Gatorade. Gatorade has a lot of sodium in it, and it was not the best choice, but at least he would take little sips of it. We were sitting together on the couch, and I was so scared because he hardly had any blood pressure and was extremely light-headed.

"Mom, am I going to die?" Christopher asked.

"I don't know, Christopher," I said with tears running down my face. "We are going to Seattle tomorrow, and I am praying Dr. Fishbein has some good ideas."

Chapter 3

Goofball and His Family

It was called the "Blob." When configured into clay by a six-year-old boy's hands, it looked sort of like an octopus. The "Blob" was the name Christopher gave his anxiety and fears. The child psychologist I took him to helped my son name this amorphous, dark presence in an otherwise normal upbringing and family. By age six Christopher's panic was already disrupting his life, preventing him from going to other friends' houses, and sometimes grabbing him at school.

As a little boy, Christopher became panicky in a store if I momentarily moved out of sight. He seemed sure at any moment I would disappear, and he would be alone forever. No amount of reassurance was ever enough for Christopher to feel comfortable without the presence of his father, brother, or mother.

Christopher came into this world a month overdue on October 20, 1981. My labor was only two hours long, and thirty minutes of that was waiting for the doctor to get to the hospital through pea soup fog. The nurses had told me, "Just lie on your side, and if you feel the need to push, let us know. We will deliver this baby without the doctor." The overwhelming need to push that I had felt when I had Jeff never came, though, and when the doctor finally appeared, I had to force myself to push. It was as if Christopher never wanted to come out, and my body didn't want to let go of him either.

When talking with the psychologist about Christopher's fears, I guiltily brought up two incidents. The first was a trip my husband and

I took when Christopher was one. My sister agreed to take our two boys for five days so Tom and I could have a "rekindling the marriage" trip. My sister told us all went well, but later she admitted Christopher was fearful a good part of the time. The second incident was a serious lapse in judgment on my part that went down in family history. Christopher later wrote vividly about this in an English essay in high school:

> *Mom Left Me!*
>
> *I could hear the thumping, rustling sounds of a school day beginning as my brother got up. The telltale sizzling pops of a fried egg in the kitchen sent its sounds more than its smells down the hall. I rolled over and down out of my warm bed. I began the long toddle down the hall in my Winnie-the-Pooh pajama suit. I was clutching my all-important blankie, DeeDee. My pajama's built-in grippy feet made their usual sticky sounds as I reached the linoleum. I was three years old.*
>
> *"Good morning, honey!" was the greeting I heard as I entered the kitchen on that foggy morning. My mother and big brother, Jeff, were going through the daily motions of getting him ready for school. Shortly after I had screeched a chair out of its resting place and climbed to the top, a piping hot bowl of Cream of Wheat was placed in front of me. It was to be used dually as food and more importantly entertainment. As my older brother gobbled down the last few morsels of his fried egg, my mother chimed in. "OK, Jeff, go get your backpack, and I'll take you to the bus."*
>
> *Jeff complied, and then Mom, the center of my whole universe, bent down before me and said, "I'm sorry, honey, but you can't come to the bus stop this morning. I have to pick up Ivey and Abel, but Mommy will be back in a few minutes."*

I immediately protested, but my mother was firm. Our car was tiny, and we wouldn't all fit. This was a big change in our normal routine, and I was worried.

By three I knew taking Jeff to the bus entailed driving down our quarter-mile driveway, waiting for a few minutes for the "Banana," as I like to call the big yellow bus, turning around, and coming home. All in all the process should have taken roughly ten minutes. Mom walked out the door with Jeff in tow, hopped in the car, and puttered out of view. I heard the crackle of the gravel as it unwillingly conformed to the will of the tire. I listened to the sounds fade into the mist, and I did a Carl Lewis toddler sprint through the living room and out to the back porch to catch a last fleeting glance of Mom's car as it passed behind a wall of Scotch broom fronds. I listened intently to the gravel pops until there was only abundant silence. I waited patiently on that deck like a castle sentry for an attacking army. All my senses were trained in the direction of the far end of the road.

Several minutes passed, and my patience began to evaporate into panic. The utter helplessness of my situation struck me like a blow to the head, and I began to pace. My sobs escalated with my surging panic. A crazy, racing train of thought plowed its way through my mind with every horrible eventuality a toddler is capable of conjuring. A car wreck in this train car. My mother murdered on this one. The thought that maybe she had just left me hung in the caboose. This scared me the most, so this was, of course, what I thought had happened. This resolution greatly multiplied my fears and was what finally drove me to action.

I booked it to the closet where my black rubber boots with red toes resided, and as best as I could by myself, I forced them on. In a split second, I was rapidly waddling my way to grab my coat and then to the toy closet to grab my trusty Uzi water gun. I did my best to fill it. In the midst of my young world crumbling into nothing, I struck out on my own that foggy morning. The misty gravel road might as well have been in the middle of the wilderness, but by God I had seen my mother leave that way, so I was going to follow for better or worse. The fog reduced my vision to only a few feet, and no sights or sounds of the outside world made their way through the translucent gray blanket that enveloped me. I stumbled on and on and wiped the tears away with my jacket sleeve. I was racked with uncontrollable sobs and waiting for the bogeyman with his snotty nose and bad breath to jump out and end my existence.

My resolve began to fade with each short stride, and just as I was about to lie down on the cold, damp gravel and accept my fate, I heard "pop, crack." Those faint notes somehow weaseled their way through the fog. It seemed as though I had heard those sounds in a faraway place many years before. I thought I imagined it, but no. The gravel song persisted and grew in strength. I stopped dead in my tracks. My cheeks were very hot and the neck of my jammies soaked in tears. The sounds grew. Eternity passed in those few moments. A silhouette appeared through the mist, and it gradually formed into a car, which stopped directly in front of me. The door flew open, and out of the driver's seat bolted my salvation and my world—my mother. She was crying, and Jeff, Ivey, and Abel were still in the car.

"Oh, Christopher!" Mom cried as she swept me up in her arms. "We missed the bus, so I thought we

could go down the road a little farther to catch it. We went farther and farther and no bus. I was more and more scared about you the farther away we got. So we just had to turn around and come back here to get you. I am so sorry I left you. It was the wrong thing to do. I will never do it again." She hugged me hard and kissed me all over the face.

Mom bundled me up and crammed me into the tiny blue car with the other kids, and off we went to take the kids, now late, all the way to school. Although I had no grounds for believing my mother was going to abandon me, my childhood paranoia more than compensated for any reason or logic I might have possessed. Unfortunately, because of this event, my unreasonable fear persisted for many years.

Christopher was a complicated child. He was the calmest, most angelic little baby. Then at a year we did a professional photo of the boys, and the worry in those little eyes was evident. When he was with the family, he laughed, played, loved, and cuddled, but the moment he feared separation, he was fretful, clingy, and panicked. I felt more protective of Christopher because he seemed so much more fragile than Jeff. My protectiveness went overboard many times. As Jeff now says, "Christopher liked to be taken care of, and Mom was a wonderful caregiver."

Christopher benefited from being the second child because I was so much calmer and more together as a second-time mom. I spent more time being with both my children—cuddling them, playing with them, and planning activities for them. It seemed with two there was more of a critical mass of kid to arrange life around, and I did.

I called Christopher a goofball because he had a head that looked twice the size necessary for his skinny little body. He was my constant companion, but Jeff was more outgoing. Christopher wanted Mom and home, and I ate it up. He talked early and lots, and it cracked me up to listen to this little person talk like an adult.

Christopher's health challenges started at birth. However, we did not know this for certain until he was fourteen months old. In those days there were no routine ultrasounds, and we didn't know he had had an event in utero that caused a blockage of cerebral spinal fluid and some damage to the left side of his brain. All I knew the first few days after we brought Christopher home was that he had an eerie, high-pitched cry I had been trained to associate with brain injury.

At a year Christopher was still not walking independently. He could walk fairly well, though, if I held his right hand. If I held his left hand, it was as if he couldn't start that first step. When he crawled he used his arms and his left leg but not his right one. At his five-month checkup, I asked his pediatrician about his right foot as it seemed to spasm. He said we should watch it. Our concerns grew as the months passed, and at fourteen months, we took Christopher for a complete evaluation.

It emerged that Christopher did have a right-sided weakness, but it was one of the mildest they had seen. Now that he was walking, the doctors were sure he would do quite well. They said he would trip a lot as a little boy, need an orthotic in his right shoe, and from time to time need a home exercise program reinforced by a pediatric physical therapist. He would probably never be a great athlete, but the evaluation showed that whatever had happened during his extended stay in my womb, it had not impacted his speech or intelligence. Tom and I breathed huge sighs of relief. We were deeply committed parents, and I was often fearful. As a nurse and an anxious person myself, I knew and worried about all the many things that could go wrong. Now we had word our toddler would be OK.

As a young boy, Christopher was our skinny little goofball who never posed for a photograph without making a funny face. Due to the blockage of fluid in his brain before birth, his head was larger than normal. We have a picture of him in his dad's shoes with his skinny body in a pair of tight swim trunks and his big head with wispy blond hair. He's holding a fish he had caught and refused to give up for almost two days! He would fish for hours and hours and jump up and down each and every time he caught one. Other pictures show him naked with soap crayons drawn red, blue, and yellow all over his body and racing around the house with his hair sticking straight up in a soap Mohawk. He loved to pose for pictures with his arms stretched wide and a silly grin on his face as if he was saying, "Ta-da! It's me!"

When Christopher was about three, a good friend of mine from high school came with her little boy, Daniel, to play with Christopher. While swinging together Christopher asked where Daniel lived. My friend Jackie said, "Daniel lives in Bellingham." Christopher got so excited. "Mommy, Mommy, Daniel lives where Jesus was born!"

On any kind of uneven ground, Christopher's weak right side caused him to trip frequently, and sports challenged him. In second grade he initially wanted to play baseball, so we signed him up for a team coached by a very nice man we knew who got help with the team from his brother. It turned out the brother was an angry alcoholic who believed that all these second-grade children needed was toughening up. After the first few practices, Christopher wanted to quit. I felt strongly that he had wanted to do this, we had paid money to do it, and he needed to honor this commitment. As long as I was there for every practice, he didn't panic, although he wasn't pleased with the situation.

During one practice I had to run to the other side of the very small town of Yelm to pick up his older brother. I explained to Christopher where I was going and that I would be right back, but he panicked. He practically clung to my leg as I got in the car. I told him this was silly, that I would be right back, and to go back to practice. The baseball experiment came to an end shortly after that. I couldn't stand to see Christopher so scared whether the reason was real or imagined. I understood the extreme discomfort of anxiety and panic and carried my own little bottle of Xanax in my purse in case I started having a panic attack.

Through fifth grade Christopher was very uncomfortable playing at his friends' houses. We would host the friends at our house, and few of his friends knew of his concerns. He seemed confident when in places he considered safe. Luckily school was a safe place as was his babysitter Lucille's house. He could also go to his great-grandma and great-grandpa's house for a sick day if I couldn't take the time off work.

To call Christopher loquacious was an understatement. He came out of the womb babbling. If he was physically less coordinated than his older brother, he made up for it in speech. By three he was using words that astounded his preschool teachers. Miss Linda and Miss Patty regularly told me stories of what Christopher had said that day.

He had a wicked sense of humor as he grew older, and spoofs from *South Park* were frequent. This included "Starvin' Marvin" and "Ethernopian." When hungry it was always, "Mom, I'm Starvin' Marvin!" Let's eat was, "Let's squeet!" When I would holler for him and call, "Christopher!" he would reply, "What-afer?"

No matter his physical challenges, as early as first grade Christopher was far ahead of his classmates in reading and writing. Mrs. Robinson consulted the second-grade teacher, Mrs. Higgins. They decided he was academically ahead but emotionally unprepared for second grade. He went to the second-grade classroom for reading and some of the academics, but he stayed with his age group.

Starting in fourth grade, the school district had a wonderful gifted program called "Challenge." An intense, passionate teacher named Lisa Iverson taught it. Mrs. Iverson had the students write, illustrate, bind, title, and create the cover artwork for their books. Christopher's first book was *Special Forces in Nam*. It was a typical shoot-'em-up army story. Christopher was big on conversation in his books. He was also a lousy typist. I helped by typing the story while he dictated. I learned how to punctuate anything.

Mrs. Iverson wrote, "Chris never fails to impress me with his remarkable understanding of ideas, moral issues, current events, and his incredible vocabulary. In a group of very strong students, many of whom have similar traits, Christopher continues to stand out in these areas." More telling about his emotional immaturity, however, was the following. "He has an intensity about him that he has difficulty controlling at times. He will continue to struggle off and on with the discrepancies between his level of emotional maturity and his more adult understanding, but that is just part of the unique person that is Chris."

For all Christopher's anxieties, he was confident in the classroom. In the fourth grade, he chose to teach a math class. His teacher said he did an "outstanding and conscientious job." He was a big ham in front of an audience and had the lead in the school Christmas play. He had grown from a skinny string bean into a chubby kid, and his girth and enthusiasm made him a great Santa.

In fourth grade Christopher also found the love of his life—football. One of Christopher's good friends, Zak Basher, encouraged him to try out. Zak's dad, Dave, was one of the coaches. While baseball had been a disaster and soccer not much better, Christopher was on fire with football. Here he could use his size to be a lineman, and he didn't have to be particularly coordinated if he could hit hard. He couldn't wait for practices to start each August, and he stayed engaged the entire season, which ended around Thanksgiving. Even though he hated the aerobic exercises of football practice, he did it all so he could play. Life for me during football season meant racing out of work in Olympia at 4:00 to pick up Christopher and friends and drive them to a three-hour practice three times a week. I came to love this. I used the time to run around the school track and then watch the practice. The games were an absolute blast, and the community of kids and their parents became a very tight-knit group. Crisp, clear fall Saturdays would find us at one of the nearby high school stadiums screaming at the tops of our lungs for our little football players.

At the end of each youth football season, a banquet was held, and the kids got trophies and special awards. Christopher was not the most gifted player due to his right-sided weakness, but he got awards for the most committed and for trying the hardest.

Football made him feel like a jock. Since his birthday was October 20 and smack-dab in the middle of football season, his parties from fourth through ninth grade meant inviting nearly the entire team to spend the night and play football in the dark with glow sticks. It was a lot of work feeding dinner and breakfast to about thirteen boys. As they left each year, Tom would resolutely say, "We aren't doing that again next year!" We always did.

I had the good fortune to work part-time when the kids were in elementary school, so I was able to volunteer in their classrooms. By the time both sons hit middle school, though, they made it clear that any volunteering in their school was totally unacceptable. Our daily conversations about school evaporated into a series of short grunts.

"What did you do in school today?" I would ask at dinner.

"Nothing," was the answer from both Jeff and Christopher.

Their lives outside our home became much more mysterious. They would never share anything about girls. My status of adored mom in elementary school became one of embarrassing mom during the middle school years. I was certainly not a trusted confidant.

With Tom an Eagle Scout, each son was expected at age ten to join the Scouts and not quit until the coveted Eagle award was bestowed sometime before age eighteen. Tom was a leader of troop number 208 for years, and both boys participated starting in the fifth grade—Jeff willingly and Christopher reluctantly. There were many wet, rainy camping weekends and an annual week at Scout camp that Christopher endured. There were an equal number of weekends where he got hurt and had to come home. Sprained ankles, fractured fibula, arms in splints, nosebleeds, severe cases of diarrhea—all these were partly a result of clumsiness from his right-sided weakness and partly stress. Tom always wanted him to "buck up" and get tougher, but there continued to be that little boy in Christopher that wouldn't or couldn't.

In middle school Christopher's anxiety lessened tremendously. He was now able to go overnight to friends' houses and never had an evening meltdown. He seemed to have lots of friends and invitations to do things, and I breathed a sigh of relief that the anxiety chapter of Christopher's life was now over.

In September of 1996, Christopher was very excited to enter Yelm High School as a freshman. Football practices had started in August, so he entered high school feeling confident. He again was playing with many of his old friends on the freshman team. Jeff had graduated the previous spring and was off to Washington State University, so Christopher got to move into his brother's bigger room. He spent a lot of time decorating the walls with football collages and posters to make the room his own. He was flying high. He had slimmed down after a growth spurt and was quite the handsome young man. He was actually getting a bit cocky, and more than once I wanted to tell him no one liked cocky people. I kept quiet, though. I knew this was a lesson he had to learn himself.

Painkillers and Gummi Bears

Tom and I had been high school sweethearts. We started dating our senior year and married during our senior year in college. I had run with a hard-partying crowd, and he was a student government, Eagle Scout type. He was drawn to me because I was wild. I was drawn to him for his seriousness and stability. Over the years we used to joke that I had loosened Tom up and he had settled me down. We also joked that Tom was so serious in his twenties he was going to have a huge midlife crisis. This wasn't nearly so funny when it actually happened years later.

We were good citizens, hard workers, and highly responsible young adults. We got married, graduated from college in 1975, went to work, built a house, and started a family. Jeff came along in May 1978 and Christopher in 1981. Tom worked for a general contracting firm, and I went to work in a hospital. We were the epitome of the nuclear family with a significant Gloria Steinem women's rights slant. Although I worked part-time when the kids were young, I was clear I had a big career to pursue, which I did with passion.

Our best family times as the kids grew up were boating adventures. Tom was a passionate boater, and we got our first twenty-seven-foot powerboat, the *Upkeep,* when Jeff was a year old. Next came the thirty-foot boat, the *Therapy* and then we graduated to a thirty-four-foot boat called the *Legacy* that we had for many years. Annual trips to the San Juan Islands or further north for crabbing, swimming, shrimping, trail walking, beach hanging, reading, rowing, and card game playing made up some of our fondest family memories.

Chapter 4

Please Get Better or Get Worse

I called the day before Christopher's clinic appointment at the University of Washington's heart failure clinic to ask if there was a place he could lie down in the clinic because he was so weak. The nurse I spoke to told me if Chris was that sick he needed to go to his local emergency room. When I called our local cardiologist's office, he was exasperated.

"Gail, we can't do any more for Chris here. We have done all we can. He must get to Seattle and those experts. The sooner the better. I don't understand what all this runaround has been and why they keeping telling us to treat him. Don't bring him here to St. Peter Hospital. Get him to that appointment in Seattle tomorrow."

"Should he go by ambulance if he is this sick? I can hardly get a blood pressure, and he is almost too weak to stand," I said.

"You are a cardiac-trained nurse, and you will know if he has a cardiac arrest," he said. "You know how to start CPR, and you can call nine-one-one. Just pay attention to the mile markers along the road. If you have an emergency, you can tell the medics where you are."

I started to resent being a cardiac nurse. The physicians expected me to be so clinical, calm, and cool. Do CPR on my own son? *Were they kidding me*? I had a huge knot in my stomach at the thought of a disaster happening to my son on my watch with me responsible. What if I panicked and froze? What if I did something wrong? What if I missed something crucial? That was the scariest thing of all. For someone already insecure about herself, this was overwhelming.

The next morning I went into Christopher's room to wake him. His bed wasn't all torn up like usual, and he hadn't woken during the night that I knew of. I sat on the edge of his bed and ran my hand through his hair.

"Good morning, sweetheart," I said. "How did you sleep?"

Christopher opened his eyes and stretched. "Man, I was in a coma. I really slept well."

We were both amazed because the day before he had felt horrible, and no matter how exhausted he felt, sleep never seemed to come easily or be restful.

He got out of bed, and as he walked to the bathroom, he said, "I actually feel pretty good."

He looked better than he had in days. He even ate a bit of breakfast before the three of us loaded in the car and headed to the heart failure clinic in Seattle. He slept peacefully during the one-hour ride. I meanwhile had my cell phone in my hand and was watching mile markers obsessively until we got to the hospital.

I breathed a huge sigh of relief once we arrived at the clinic. Here were people who could really help Christopher, and I could let my caregiver burden go. When Christopher's name was called, he walked into the exam room. Tom and I followed.

Dr. Fishbein came in and examined Christopher. He raised his eyebrows when he saw Chris. "Boy, you look much better than I expected. I was told your mom called yesterday to see if you could come on a stretcher." As he examined Chris, he said, "Your color is good. Your skin is warm and dry." He took his blood pressure. It was low but acceptable. "Eighty over fifty. Not bad considering the medication we have you on." He felt his ankles and pressed his fingers into the skin. "No swelling of the ankles. No weight gain from edema." He stood back and crossed his arms. "Not bad," he said. "How have you been feeling?"

"Overall pretty bad, but this morning amazingly good," Christopher said. "Sick to my stomach but thirsty. The only thing that tastes good to me is frozen Gatorade."

"Gatorade!" Dr. Fishbein said. "That is far too salty for you!"

He gave me the wilting stare of a physician to a nurse who should know better. I cringed but raised my hands in a futile gesture. "That was the only thing that sounded good to him, and he only had a little. I wouldn't have let him drink tons of it."

I shared my list of questions with Dr. Fishbein. The list included my repeated inability to hear his blood pressure and Christopher's extreme fatigue, high heart rate, light-headedness, significant side pain, abnormal breathing during sleep, nausea, and thirst. I also recounted the Olympia hospitalization and frequent doctor office visits.

"It does sound like a rough couple weeks," Dr. Fishbein said, and he looked more concerned. "I think I will take him to the echo lab and look at his heart function down there. We won't be long. You can just stay here."

Dr. Fishbein went to the echo lab with Chris in a wheelchair, and Tom and I waited in the exam room. As we waited for Christopher to return, I told Tom in a panicked tone, "What if he sends him back home? I wish he looked as bad today as he has been looking. He has to stay here. He is going to die if he doesn't."

I absolutely knew this in my heart. I was wringing my clammy hands and trying to slow my breathing so my heart wouldn't beat out of my chest. How was a mother supposed to deal with this? I asked this question to God then and often thereafter.

Tom said through gritted teeth, "Gail, I have been praying for two outcomes—that Christopher either gets well or worse. I want him totally well or bad enough he needs a heart transplant. I can't stand the thought of him chronically ill with a horrible quality of life. That's not good for Christopher or our family. We need to *do* something."

Tom was right. I knew from my cardiac nursing experience that heart failure in its worst form was a miserable condition that left the patient feeling exhausted most of the time. There were severe restrictions to activity and diet, and Christopher would hate all that. We were an active family, and this would have destroyed quality of life for all of us.

Therefore, there was actually some relief when Dr. Fishbein returned looking quite alarmed. "Christopher's heart is barely functioning.

Without immediate intervention he is not going to survive. I am admitting him to the cardiac intensive care unit, and I am putting him on the cardiac transplant list as a priority one patient."

"What does priority one mean?" I asked, hoping it meant immediate help.

"Priority one, or 'Status One A,' means the patient has a life expectancy without a heart transplant of fourteen days or less. When any heart from Texas to the West Coast becomes available, he will be the first one evaluated to receive it," Dr. Fishbein stated hurriedly. "In the meantime we are going to place a large intravenous catheter into the side of his neck. This will give us continuous information about the pressure in his lungs and heart as well as his heart's output. Medication will go into that IV to improve his heart function. I will go the ICU and write the orders. The nurse will escort you to the cardiac ICU."

It probably seems odd to say this decision energized and relieved us, but it did. It was a huge turning point. I was no longer taking care of a dying child at home. The past two weeks had been the worst kind of hell for a mother. I had been in medical limbo between Olympia and the UW, and I had felt totally alone. I had been running around with my hair on fire and screaming that my son was dying, but it felt as if no one had been listening.

To have Dr. Fishbein finally confirm what I had known in my heart—that Christopher was on death's doorstep—was a total relief in that moment. I was terrified about the road ahead, but at least we *had* a road. We had a plan at a highly regarded heart transplant hospital, and serendipitously we were in the hands of one of the best heart failure specialists in the United States. We had a plan and caregivers who knew far better than I how to take care of our son. While seriously concerned for Christopher, I was almost giddy with relief. My care burden as a nurse was relinquished, and I could be a 100 percent supportive mom—the role I most wanted to play.

Without a medical background, Tom had almost no idea what we were up against. He saw a cure and wanted it with his whole heart. As a father he wanted to protect his family. This was his deep and primal instinct. He had felt totally helpless and increasingly distraught as Christopher faded.

This much was starkly clear—a heart transplant was Christopher's only chance of living. I thanked God repeatedly for this opportunity. This was Christopher's life ring. It was thrown from the only boat that could save his life, and we grabbed it because we were all drowning.

"Dr. Fishbein," Tom asked, "why does he look so good today when he is actually so ill?"

"I think his lack of fluid intake the past few days has kept the pressure off his heart for this short time," the doctor replied. "The echo, however, shows how ineffective his heart function actually is. Often the presenting symptom of cardiomyopathy in children is sudden death because young bodies can compensate so much better than older bodies. This disease can show very few symptoms until it is too late. It is very lucky for Christopher you came today."

"I was so worried you might send him home again," I said breathlessly. Tears of relief were running down my face. "I am relieved he is going to an ICU that knows how to take care of someone so sick. Olympia doesn't see kids this sick, and I have been at my wit's end. Thank you!" I wiped the tears with the back of my hand. The relief of no longer being Christopher's caregiver flowed from me.

"OK. Let's do this thing," Tom said as he shook Dr. Fishbein's hand. "I have felt so helpless these past few weeks. Now I feel as if we have a plan, and Christopher has a chance for a healthy life."

Christopher had not returned with Dr. Fishbein, so we heard the news of how severely ill he was and his priority one heart transplant status without him present. Everything happened so fast that day. I didn't even know what Christopher had been told, but a few minutes later, he wheeled by us on his gurney with stark terror in his eyes. He grabbed my arm like a vise grip, and tears ran down his face.

"I hate that echo lab," he said. "I can't breathe when they put me flat. I don't want to go to the ICU. I am so freaked out right now I can hardly breathe. You and Dad are not leaving me for even a second," he said in an angry and frightened voice.

Both his dad and I kissed and hugged him and assured him we were all in this together. We wouldn't leave his side.

Chapter 5

Heart Transplant Required—Pretty Freaked Out

We followed Christopher as his stretcher was wheeled into the cardiac ICU. Four medical people descended on him. "What's your name?" one of them asked.

"How are you feeling?" asked another as they let down the side of the gurney and slid him onto the ICU bed.

"Pretty freaked out," Christopher replied.

"Can he have something to calm him down? He is extremely panicked," I said.

"His heart rate is certainly up there," said one of the nurses.

Anxiety produces adrenaline, and that increases heart rate—not a good thing in a sick, compromised heart.

"How much do you weigh?" one asked Christopher.

"About two hundred," Christopher said.

"Give him two milligrams Ativan IV push," stated the physician.

Although a standard dose in a large, distressed person, it was too much for Christopher. He became momentarily unconscious, and his blood pressure dropped to a dangerously low level.

"There goes his blood pressure," a nurse said in a tense, hurried tone. "Putting on some oxygen and opening up his IV fluids."

"Come on. Come on, Chris. Get that blood pressure back," she cajoled gently while shaking him.

It was obvious the nurses were worried but trying not to let on with his parents right there. Luckily the peak effect of the medication was brief, but it was a very scary few minutes until it started wearing off and Christopher came around. He opened his eyes and scanned the room with much less anxiety.

"That's better," said a relieved nurse.

Christopher was then assigned a nurse named Ian. Ian was a blond, athletic young man with a good tan and short, spiky hair. He had an air of confidence bordering on cockiness, but he was easygoing, and Christopher related to him right away.

"Hey, man, what do you like to do when you aren't sick?" Ian asked Chris.

"I like to ride my mountain bike, play football, and I ski." Chris grunted this answer. "What about you?"

"I am an avid snowboarder, but my favorite sport is street luge," Ian said as he reached over to work with one of several IV fluid pumps.

"Rad," said Chris.

"What is street luge?" I said with a puzzled look on my face. I had heard of luge in the Olympics but not street luge.

"It's when you ride down steep hills lying on something like a large skateboard," Ian said with an impish grin.

"Oh my God. That sounds so dangerous," I said.

"It is totally an adrenaline rush," said Ian.

I started out as an ICU nurse and had met many nurses like Ian who were adrenaline junkies. They lived for thrills and the feeling of being on the edge all the time. Not having that kind of personality, I had burned out in the ICU after eighteen months and had to find a less intense place to work. Ian was totally in the flow of his work, and the pride he took in the exacting but stressful job of titrating Christopher's medications was obvious.

Over the course of the afternoon, Ian constantly monitored Chris's condition and adjusted his medication. They talked about skiing, snowboarding, skateboarding, and young "guy" talk. I was quietly thanking God for the connection these two had made and for Christopher now being in the hands of the expert University of Washington cardiac program.

Christopher was taken to diagnostic imaging, and a large-bore IV catheter called a Swan-Ganz catheter was inserted in the side of his neck. The end of this catheter floated close to the heart so pressure readings could be taken and cardiac output could be measured. Both were indications of heart function. With these measurements taken hourly or more, Ian was able to titrate microdoses of two powerful IV drugs that worked in combination to improve heart function. One of these was the drug the Olympia cardiologist had tried but in too large a dose. Over the evening we could see Christopher perk up as if being raised from the nearly dead.

By the next morning, he had a huge smile on his face and felt as if he was healed. "I am going to beat this," he said. "Now where is some breakfast? 'Cause I am hungry!"

With that the cardiac care unit became our family home. From the first day, Christopher insisted on wearing his own shirts and shorts. My parents, Grandma Audrey and Grandpa Larry, donated a king-size down pillow in a bright pink polka-dot pillowcase. He had colorful cards and banners all over the walls.

"Christopher, it isn't always going to be possible to get T-shirts on with that monstrous IV and all those wires coming out of your neck," I said. "How about we get you some button-up shirts?"

"OK," Christopher said reluctantly. "But make Jeff pick them out because you and Dad will pick something gross. And make them short-sleeved. It is hot as a mother in here most of the time."

One day he donned a cloth mask like the nurses wore to change his IV dressing. He put on my bright pink tanning booth eye protectors and lay there giving us all the peace sign until the nurse came back in. At other times it wasn't the peace sign but the finger. It depended on his mood.

Christopher was an anomaly at University Hospital. They hadn't had a fifteen-year-old there before. They were used to consenting, compliant adults anxious to do what the doctor said. After about a week of daily academic rounds at 7:00 a.m. when a dozen medical people barged into his room and surrounded his bed to examine him and discuss his condition, Christopher rebelled.

"This is ridiculous!" he said self-righteously. "We are sick people and need our sleep. They all wake us up at the Effing crack of dawn and stand around the bed. I hardly get any sleep, and the mornings are when I want to sleep!" He went on. "One doctor can come in to examine me in the morning, but the rest have to stay in the hall. Mom, you tell them they have to meet outside my room!"

I timidly made this request to the nurse, and the nurse passed it on to Dr. Fishbein. He was kind enough to grant Christopher's wish. In addition Christopher wanted his door and window blinds closed at all times. I felt claustrophobic in his room.

"Christopher, you look like a hermit!" I told him. "I can't stand it so dark in here all the time. It is depressing enough you are stuck in here. Can't we let in the sunlight? It makes me feel so much better," I said.

"Mom, who is the patient here?" Christopher replied. "Who can't leave this flippin' room?"

"I know, sweetheart," I said, "but you also want one of us in here with you at all times, so I am just asking we compromise and let some light in at times."

"Obo-kaybe," Christopher relented. "Sometimes. Not all the time."

"Obo-kaybe" was a word Jeff created when he was a little kid. It meant "OK" and became a family expression. I leaned over the head of his bed and hugged him the best I could. I felt a huge wave of love and understanding for this wonderful child who was trying hard to consider my needs as well as his own.

The medical team was very kind to me and allowed me to stand in at rounds each morning. The plan from day one was to stabilize Christopher's heart on the IV medications. The second step was to transition him to oral medications to see if he could get well enough to wait for his new heart at home.

When he first heard about waiting for a new heart, Christopher refused to believe this. He was convinced he was going to get well and wouldn't need a heart transplant.

As long as the IV medication was working well, Christopher felt great, and he was not willing to accept the doctors' predictions that his heart would not heal. Within a few days, though, we received a three-ring binder called "Heart and Lung Transplantation." The clinical educator told me to read a little at a time to keep from getting overwhelmed.

After rounds the next morning, Dr. Fishbein confided in me. "Christopher's chances of having a good quality of life for up to fifteen years with a heart transplant are very good."

He said this as if this was very good news, and it certainly would have been if Christopher was already old. From the beginnings of heart transplant surgery in 1967, initial survival rates measured in months. Fifteen years was outstanding, but my son was still only fifteen years old.

I was supposed to be happy with my fifteen-year-old having fifteen more years of life. Was he kidding me? That meant living to thirty as a best-case scenario. *I couldn't stand that.* My heart began pounding, I was shaking, and I thought I would faint and throw up at the same time. Scenes of standing over my son's casket filled my head, and I immediately dismissed this thought. I silently shouted every obscenity. I refused to believe this was true. It couldn't be true, and I couldn't breathe. How was a mother supposed to deal with this kind of news about her son? The idea of outliving my son, even in the best medical scenario, was incomprehensible.

How would we tell this to Christopher? *No! No! No!* That was all I could think. I was in the hall outside Christopher's room when I received this information, and I knew I had to go back in there and act as if nothing catastrophic had happened. I can't remember the rest of that day, but somehow I got through it without imparting my terror or sorrow to Christopher.

Christopher made it clear he did not expect to spend one second waiting in the ICU for a new heart without a family member present, and we didn't want him to be alone. That meant every single minute there except for showers and runs to the cafeteria. Tom always found comfort in certainty and was fond of scheduling, so he devised a calendar of who would be at the hospital and when. It was complete with colors to highlight each person's role.

My boss had granted me a leave of absence for up to a year, so I had the most available time. Tom had started a business in January with a fellow general contractor, and he needed to work at least half-time. Jeff was home from college after finals by the end of the first week of May, so he was penciled into the schedule also. I would have preferred to never leave Christopher's side, but Tom and Jeff kicked me out. They wanted time with him, and space was limited. A bed chair was brought in, and the UW staff was marvelous about letting us stay. We showered across the hall in a patient shower, and we did our best to keep our clothing bags tucked into several little cubbies on the north side of the room. We also had cookies, cards, books, magazines, and other items to help us pass the time. This was long before portable video games, iPads, and smartphones. Frequently we were all there together in the evenings and on weekends.

One night several days into his ICU stay, Christopher was left alone for a few minutes while I took a shower. When I returned he was freaked out because he was sure the chair had talked to him. He realized it was a hallucination, but it seemed so real to him. Losing control of his mind was one more blow to his already diminished sense of who he was—up until recently a healthy, normal fifteen-year-old freshman in high school.

Christopher usually stayed up until midnight when he had his only peaceful few hours. After all the midnight vital signs were taken, he was given one milligram of Ativan for sleep. This was the only time he could forget where he was and how sick he was and let go of worry. I would watch him get a smile on his face and fade into sleep. I watched his heart rate slow a bit. I was also thankful for this respite. We had a CD player in the room and always put on our favorite George Winston CD with its peaceful, soft music. I would snuggle into my chair bed, say my prayers, and lie there thinking about the day. Sometimes I would be wound up so tightly I couldn't sleep or would sleep fitfully. Other times I would fall into the deep sleep of exhaustion.

Christopher never ate the patient's food. Never. Sometimes we ate it but never Christopher. I went to the cafeteria to get him food, or else I'd bring something in from a local restaurant. The physicians decided early on (thank God) they were not going to restrict his salt intake, but instead they would monitor his weight and increase his diuretics to cover whatever "salt weight" was gained. He got so many potent diuretics that he had an almost constant infusion of potassium. (Diuretics greatly deplete this vital electrolyte.) The doctors knew so much had already been taken away from Christopher—his health, independence, and mobility—that they let him eat what he wanted.

I actually loved taking his order for the day and going wherever the heck he ordered from to bring back this treat. This was one small pleasure he had, and I got to do it for him. There was little else I could do to make things better.

While living in the ICU at University Hospital, we received a touching letter from the emergency room physician at Pullman Memorial Hospital who had initially diagnosed Christopher's heart failure.

Dear Gail Stewart,

Please accept my apologies for not responding sooner to your very thoughtful thank-you letter. Since I only work at Pullman one weekend a month, I did not receive your letter until June. Then it was the normal summer craziness, and to be honest I guess I have been somewhat afraid to write because I didn't want to hear any bad news.

I think of Christopher often and Jeff as well because I have sons who are twenty-two and nineteen and also close friends. It was touching to witness Jeff's concern for his younger brother, to talk to you and your family on the phone, and to feel the love you have for one another.

Medicine, as you know, can be filled with great rewards of helping others, but it can also be filled with great sadness at times in our inability to achieve the outcome we desire.

I would appreciate hearing a report of Christopher's condition because I am hopeful the news is good and I can share in your joy. If, on the other hand, you have sad news to report, I can also share in your grief.

One of my favorite sayings is, "A joy shared is a doubled joy, and a sorrow shared is but half a sorrow."

Please communicate my concern and respect to your husband, Jeff, and others with whom I conversed during those frightening hours in April.

With compassion and hoping to hear a positive report, I am your friend.

Wm. Lamont Worden, MD

One of the medical residents on Christopher's team was an Earth Mother type who felt strongly that Christopher needed fresh air and time outside the ICU, so she wrote an order for him to be taken outside. It was May, and the weather was wonderful. Our first "field trip" was heavenly. The nurse took Christopher and his IV pole to a deck overlooking the Montlake Cut—an artificial channel between Lake Washington and Lake Union. It was warm and lovely. It was a freeing and uplifting experience, and Christopher couldn't wait to do it again. Another time we took him down to the back entrance of the lower level of the hospital to visit our two dogs. It was an emotional reunion. The dogs went crazy when they saw all of us, and Christopher had tears streaming down his face as he petted Amber and Shadow.

When Dr. Fishbein found out Christopher had gone off the floor and even outside, he was very upset. He overrode the medical resident's order with his own that stated Christopher could only go outside if emergency equipment accompanied him. This increased the hassle of an outside field trip exponentially, and we went out only one more time.

Painkillers and Gummi Bears

By the third week in the ICU, Christopher was declining emotionally and physically. The plan continued to be to try to stabilize Christopher's heart function with the IV drips and then transition him to oral medication so he could go home to wait for a new heart. Christopher felt so good with the initial level of IV medication, he was certain his heart was healing. Each time the IV medication was decreased and the oral medication was introduced, it was as if we could watch his life slowly drain. His healthy skin tone would begin to pale, his blood pressure would drop, his fatigue and light-headedness would return, his appetite would wane, and food would make him nauseated. The weaning was attempted at least three times before it was decided Christopher was absolutely dependent on the IV drip medications and would have to stay in the ICU until a heart was found.

As the weeks wore on, Christopher refused to believe he needed a heart transplant —even when his body was repeatedly telling him otherwise. Reality hit him full-on the day the cardiac surgeon came to his room. This bigger-than-life woman swept into the room and introduced herself as Christopher's heart transplant surgeon. It wasn't so much what she said but simply her presence that told Christopher all hope of healing his own heart was gone. He would have to go forward into this medical hell he was trying so hard to pretend wasn't happening.

The cardiac surgeon only stayed a few minutes. When she left things were very still for a moment, and Christopher wouldn't even look at me. He was obviously upset, and tears were streaming down his face. He was so angry.

Christopher put his headphones on, cranked up a hard rock CD, and shut out the world. He put a pillow over his face and would not talk to or acknowledge anyone for several hours. I wanted to go over and hold him, but from his body language I knew I had to stay away.

Christopher's health was obviously declining. The IV medications were not working as well, and one of them, nitroprusside, was building up in the body and would have to be stopped soon. Morning rounds took on a quieter, more concerned tone. Christopher had lost almost thirty pounds, which was not entirely bad. His heart did not have so much body mass to perfuse, but malnutrition took a toll in other ways. Even Christopher was coming to terms with a heart transplant in his future. Once he accepted this, he wanted to get on with it. Memorial Day weekend was coming up, and the nurses raised our hopes that a heart might come available over this holiday weekend from "donorcycles"—what they grimly called motorcycles.

It was May 30—the night of Jeff's nineteenth birthday gathering at the hospital. Christopher looked tired and thin, and he had dark circles under his eyes. He was trying to laugh and joke with his and Jeff's friends, but there was an undeniable distance and sadness. My mom saw it too, and we were hard-pressed to keep up the illusion of happiness, even though we very much wanted Jeff to enjoy his birthday time and have a few moments in the spotlight. When the party in the hospital cafeteria was over, it was Jeff's turn to stay the night, so Tom and I headed home.

Tom and I got home to Olympia and climbed into bed together—a rare treat in those days. We were nodding off when the phone rang at 11:50 p.m. It was Jeff calling to tell us Nurse Ian had heard Dr. Fishbein being paged. There were rumblings a heart might be available.

We were both instantly awake with excitement and panic. Jeff said the doctors would call when they had more information. Tom and I looked at each other and knew we couldn't sleep. We told Jeff we were going to head up to the hospital but to call us if it was a false alarm.

As we passed Tacoma, my cell phone rang. It was Jeff excitedly telling us there was a heart, and Christopher was one of two patients in ICU who were being prepped. The actual prep would take several hours, and Christopher had gone downstairs for some tests. We continued driving to Seattle and got there about 1:00 a.m. Nurse Ian was flying around trying to get all the preoperative transplant protocol done. We were laughing, joking, hugging, and touching. We were tearing up and having every emotion possible.

Our excitement lasted until about four in the morning when things settled down. It was important Christopher try to get some sleep. Jeff had the sleeper chair, Tom was in a straight-backed chair, and I was on the floor against the wall and squished around the exercise bike.

The rumor from Ian was that the donor was at Harborview Medical Center, but the heart's size was a concern. The donor was female and quite a bit smaller than Christopher. There was also discussion that the full grown heart might still grow with Christopher. He was fifteen and had a lot of growth hormone circulating. The transplant surgeon wanted to see the size of the heart before deciding which patient would receive it.

Sandy Kruse, one of two nurses who worked with the cardiologists, came to the room and stated that we needed to sign the informed consent. In a consulting room at five in the morning with those neon lights that wash the life out of anything and anyone, Sandy explained in stark detail the risks of the procedure. It was one thing to know as a cardiac nurse that this was a risky surgery. It was quite another as a mother to hear the high percentage of deaths, infections, and strokes that resulted from heart transplants. On the other hand, clearly Christopher was going to die without a new heart. Tom and I both knew that. We had no choice but to sign the consent, and sign we did. The question about how a mother was supposed to handle something like this returned. The answer came immediately. It was not comforting, but it was true. I had no other choice, so I sucked it up and did it.

We went back into the darkened room where Jeff and Chris were sleeping and fell into fitful, uncomfortable sleep. At 7:30 a.m. the transplant team came flying into the room. The decision was made, and Christopher was chosen to receive the heart. Christopher, who had been amazingly calm most of the night, took on a wide-eyed, apprehensive demeanor. I grabbed Christopher's hand and didn't let go.

The time came to take him to surgery. We all rode down in the patient elevator and said our good-byes outside the operating room doors. Christopher had already been given something to relax him. We leaned over the railings and hugged and kissed as best we could with the huge IV catheter coming out of his neck. We all told Christopher how much we loved him, and off he went into the OR. By the time we got to the surgery waiting room, a crowd of family and friends were gathering. The next time we saw our son, he would have a new heart.

Chapter 6

Heart Transplant

It was the weekend, and the corridors were quiet. The silence felt right. There are no words to explain the reverence of that moment as we experienced it in the hospital early that Saturday morning. One person's life was ending, and patients on death's doorstep were being given chances at lives because of this death. Everyone felt the sacredness.

The donor was a thirty-one-year-old healthy woman who was able to donate most of her organs. Prayers of the most extreme gratitude along with fervent prayers to have my son make it through the surgery were in my heart and on my lips all day. Family and close friends joined us, and we all kept touching and holding each other. We wiped our tears and quietly laughed at remembered family stories. We were part of an awesome event that day, and we spoke in hushed tones as if in a cathedral.

A holy presence was palpable in the surgery waiting room. We looked across the room to a family huddled together. They were waiting while their loved one received a liver. Across the hall was another family also benefiting from this death. The magnitude of this gift was overwhelming to all of us.

The donor was brought into an operating room on life support, and the plan was for a surgical team to harvest the organs while Christopher was in one operating room and the patient receiving the liver was in another.

Painkillers and Gummi Bears

At about 11:00 a.m., we heard they had removed Christopher's heart. He was on the bypass machine now. The thought of my child lying in an operating room with his chest cavity open and no heart was surreal and scary. My son's innocence, freedom, and all hopes of a normal life had just been removed with his heart. His only hope for any life was contingent on the new heart. There was absolutely no turning back, and an unknown future lay ahead. I shivered. The doctors later told us Christopher could not have lived more than a few days with his own heart. It was horribly damaged and dilated.

The next news we received was about two hours later. The new heart was almost in place. The critical part was to get Christopher off the bypass machine and start the new heart beating. That call didn't come for what seemed like a very long time, and we were beginning to panic. Apparently it took quite a bit of doing to get the new heart going in Christopher's chest.

At the end of the surgery (a total of more than six hours), we were told Christopher would be sent to the ICU directly instead of to the recovery room. Two nurses would be caring for him for several hours. The immediate family—Jeff, Tom, and I—could only visit for a few moments.

We all had to don gowns, gloves, and masks to be able to go in to see him. We gathered around the bed. Christopher still had the breathing tube in and was hooked to a ventilator. He had an unbelievable amount of equipment connected to him, and he couldn't yet move from the anesthetic. He looked pale, cold, and barely alive. My husband leaned over to Christopher's ear and said, "Christopher, the sex change operation was successful!"

We cracked up, but the nurse in charge didn't think we were funny at all. She glared at us. Christopher moved his little finger just a tiny bit to let us know he heard us, and I think he appreciated Tom's joke.

Then we had to leave. A large group of us went to the original Red Robin, which was across the Montlake Cut from the hospital. Tom and I bought everyone lunch and drinks. We were toasting over and over again as we ate lunch. Everyone was euphoric the surgery was over and successful.

Months later Christopher described the night he got the news of his heart transplant operation in an essay he wrote for a class:

"The sounds of Nintendo were being drowned out by the adrenaline roar in my head. All things took on a surrealistic feel. The magnitude of the information, which I had heard not five minutes before, had more impact than anything I had ever heard.

I sat there in the hospital bed with my eyes locked upon a video game I wasn't paying attention to. All the now-familiar sounds seemed very distant. The IV medication infuser's gentle sounds and the cool feeling of the medication entering my bloodstream seemed almost serene. The innumerable tubes that clung to my body like vines twenty-four hours a day seemed strangely bearable. I stared around at what had served as my home for the last month. I looked at the get-well cards that filled every square inch of the wall and the collection of machines that kept me alive. My palms got sweaty, and a tremor ran through my body. The intense reality of the moment blew me away. Suddenly my mind was more active than ever before. Not until I felt the prospect of being relieved of this clinical hell in which I resided did I realize how truly sick I was. My brain was trying desperately to grasp that I was overjoyed, more afraid than I had ever been, and in complete disbelief. I was struck by the complete undeniable fact of my own mortality. The chance I might not see another day made me entirely and completely alone.

When Ian, my nurse, entered the room, we knew what he was going to say. My brother and I had known from the moment the phone rang. My adrenaline sky-rocketed with the anticipation of the news. Ian quickly walked into the room and tried to be professional.

"Now don't get too excited," he said, "but that was the doctor, and we could have a heart donor."

I closed my eyes and listened while he continued to explain what would be done to determine if I was a viable recipient or not. All I could do was nod. What was I supposed to do? My consciousness was flooded by the indelible image of my cold body lying on the operating room table with the almost cliché high-pitched whine of a heart monitor proclaiming to all my life was over. This was the moment I had been anticipating for two months, and I was more unprepared than I could have ever possibly imagined.

The nurses came and went. They took blood for innumerable tests and did hundreds of things. They were seemingly as prepared for this event as I was unprepared. Time crawled by. My parents arrived and offered what little support they could. Bags upon bags of toxic medications were pumped into my system. My mind and body, exhausted from the events and adrenaline of the previous few hours, fell into a fitful sleep.

I awoke, and all was silent. During my sleep they must have finished their tasks. The lights were off, and various family members were strewn about my room. The hum of the monitors and the persistent groan of the infusers coupled with the familiar sounds of the always-busy hallway. This sent me back into my fitful slumber. My mind struggled to understand that, even though I was very much alive at the moment, I might never smell a freshly cut lawn again, have the simple luxury of sleeping in my own bed, or see my mother's face again. The reality of the situation was too much, and I quietly and softly cried myself to sleep. My weak, sickened heart continued to attempt to perform a function it was no longer capable of.

At 7:15 a.m. Dr. Jones entered the room and said, "It's a go!"

My bed was wheeled out of my room and through the bustling halls. My mind was screaming. Do you have any clue what's about to be done to me? I might never wake up. Don't you care? They rolled me into the surgery suite—another room devoid of humanity. I was informed it was time to say good-bye for what very well could be the last time. A nurse gave me a relaxant, and almost immediately I felt a warm numbness envelop my body. At that moment my mind gave up all hope of trying to understand what was happening. For the first time in fourteen hours, I was calm.

My preconception of what an operating room was like was five or so people in a fairly large room with an operating table. That was exceeded one hundred fold. The lights were intensely bright as I was rolled into the room. Fifteen people were scurrying about doing God knows what to what seemed like more machines than any single medical procedure should ever need. With my limited knowledge, I was able to identify the heart–lung bypass machine as well as a few others. It seemed as though my arrival went unnoticed for the first few seconds, but then, as though in the middle of a feeding frenzy, I was swarmed. A stream of needles entered my arms. Through the increasing fog of pre-operative medications, the preparations for my surgery made less and less sense. The last words I heard were, "We're giving you something to put you to sleep now. I want you to count backward from ten."

A warm feeling. A hum in the ears. Ten, nine, eight, seven…blackness.

Through the nothingness came the slightest sound. It was not a mechanical noise and not an unfamiliar sound but a slow, methodical murmur. It seemed as though I should have been able to understand it. Try as I might, I could not. As time passed more sounds began invading the blackness. Intense fear gripped me. Was I dead? Was this hell? Heaven? What was going on? What had happened? Thousands of other questions raced through my consciousness. Then the odd but strangely familiar sounds began to take shape. The murmurs began to have slightly different tones and cadences. My mind reached through the dense fog and pulled out the realization that the sounds were voices. I was elated. Dead or not, the sound of another voice gave me hope. I tried to cry out and let whomever or whatever know that he, she, or it was not alone, but I couldn't speak. I tried to move or do something but to no avail.

As time passed my mind began to clear away the haze bit by bit. I remembered a hospital, nurses, and being sick. But why? I pondered this question, and as though a door had opened, it dawned on me—heart transplant. I slowly became aware of the tube down my throat, the bed beneath me, and the pain. I was alive! The realization hit me like a Mack truck. I thanked God, my family, modern medicine, and every other thing I could think of.

I was not happy for long, though. As soon as I understood the pain, it increased exponentially. It felt as though every inch of my body had been torn apart and hastily reassembled without paying attention to the instructions.

Through the drugs, pain, and paralysis came a voice that for all intents and purposes was an angel. My nurse said, "Christopher, the operation went very well. Just relax, and everything's going to be OK."

I had beaten the Grim Reaper at his own game. I was alive!

Dr. Fishbein never allowed family members to stay in the room after heart transplant surgery due to the high risk of infection. In Christopher's case, however, the surgery chief resident (a mother herself) overruled him. One of us could sleep in the room, but the person had to wear an isolation gown, gloves, hat, and mask. I spent the first night. It was miserable trying to sleep with all the lights on in a mask and gloves, but I would have done anything to be close to my son.

In the old ICU room, we were used to eating in the room and keeping all our clothing, family items, cards, and posters, but that could not happen in this room. It was so cold and bare. I seriously hated that room. Every time we wanted to eat or even sip coffee, we had to go out and then put on new gloves, foot covers, gowns, masks, and hair covers to reenter.

Christopher's breathing tube was removed the next day. He had two small temporary pacemaker wires coming out of his chest, tubes to reinflate his lungs, and a drainage tube to take off the fluid around the surgical site. He had IVs with medication that wiped out his immune system so he would not reject the new heart that was foreign to his body. He was highly susceptible to any infection, hence the isolation room with the anteroom and all the gloves, gowns, and other precautions.

By day four Christopher's new heart still was not beating on its own, and there were a few comments about a permanent pacemaker being needed if the heart didn't start its own rhythm soon. Finally at 8:28 p.m. on June 4, Christopher's new heart started beating on its own. The nurse was kind enough to save the EKG strip, and I have it in a scrapbook still today.

Initially the heart function was good. Then it started getting slowly worse. The numbers indicating how Christopher's heart was pumping were not encouraging, his urine output was low, and he was retaining fluid. Concerns surfaced that the heart size might be too small. We all knew the heart was smaller and from a woman, and Christopher, though only fifteen, had a big man's body. They used this heart because it matched his tissue type but also because Christopher had been failing and only days away from death. There was also concern there might be early rejection of the organ, so he had to have a heart biopsy to show this was not the case.

They severely restricted Christopher's fluids. He could only have four cups in twenty-four hours. This was horrible. Christopher was so miserable with his postoperative pain, weakness after so many days in bed, nausea from the medications, swollen legs, and lack of progress, and the fluid restriction nearly put him over the edge of anger and despair. All the nerve fibers from his old heart had been severed and nothing reconnected. The body was screaming to the brain, "I am dying from blood loss. Get me some fluids!" We were told the postoperative thirst would be huge, miserable, and insatiable. Those few days before Christopher started peeing were the lowest of his postoperative stay. The immunosuppression pills he had to take were "horse pills." It took almost all his fluids to get these pills down. Christopher was so angry that the tiny bit of fluid he was allowed each day had to be used to swallow pills.

After a few days of worsening numbers, the medical team was growing quite somber. One of Dr. Fishbein's partners covering for him on the weekend had an idea there might be an accumulation of fluid in the pericardial sac—a baglike structure around the heart. As he described it to us, this straw-colored fluid might have accumulated in this area, as the sac was much larger than the new heart. If this was the case, it could be exerting a lot of pressure on the outside of the heart and preventing it from pumping forcefully enough to meet Christopher's bodily needs.

Christopher went down for an ultrasound. It revealed fluid, and the cardiologist drained 1100 cubic centimeters (over a quart) of fluid out of the pericardial sac. He told us if this was the problem, then Chris would start peeing like a racehorse.

Shortly after Christopher returned from this procedure and all through the night, he filled urinal after urinal—seven pounds of fluid in the first twelve hours. He hardly got any sleep because he kept waking up to pee. The next morning this cardiologist, normally a rather serious, reserved physician, was all but dancing a jig and smiling from ear to ear.

Christopher's heart function improved dramatically, and his recovery quickly advanced.

Finally on June 11 Christopher was moved out of the ICU to the less intensive step-down unit. He was encouraged to get up, walk, and sit in a chair as much as he could. Leaving the cocoon of the ICU after six weeks was incredibly hard for all of us. We were used to a nurse immediately available and took great comfort in that. There were four patients for every nurse on this nursing unit, so it felt as if we hardly saw Christopher's nurse. We felt isolated down a long corridor, even though we knew he was being monitored.

The night before Christopher was discharged, we took over a small lounge area at the end of the hall. I went to Boston Market and brought back a feast of fried chicken, mashed potatoes and gravy, green beans, and baking powder biscuits. It was the first time the four of us had eaten together as a family since April, and we were all giddy. Words can't describe the bliss of being alive and together in that moment. We laughed so hard we cried about things that would probably not bring more than a small smile today. We knew with intense certainty that our love for each other was the most important thing in the world. The little room glowed with love and warmth that night. We all stuffed ourselves and were miserably happy afterward. Discharge was the next day, and a whole new life was waiting for us outside the walls of the University of Washington Medical Center.

June 13 came, and we all were so ready to get the hell out of there. We had to wait for the last discharge instructions and the medications, which were significant and complicated—sixty pills a day for the first few months. We didn't leave until late afternoon.

Christopher was told he always had to wear a mask while in a medical facility, so he had one on as we wheeled him through the hospital lobby and out the door. Once outside he got out of the wheelchair, ripped off his mask, and inhaled deeply the fresh air of a beautiful sunny June day. The temperature was in the seventies, and he was loving that fresh air, sun, and freedom.

I brought the car up, and Christopher and Jeff got in. We rolled all the windows down and whooped and hollered as we drove toward my sister's house in Bothell.

The boys made me stop at the very first 7-11 for some junk food. Christopher refused to put on his mask in the store. He wasn't even supposed to be around anyone at that time, but he sauntered in as if it was just an average day and bought a bag of Cheetos and a Green River soda. So much for hospital food and his salt-restricted diet! That evening we had dinner with my sister and her family and reveled in being out of the hospital. We all slept in real beds without heart monitors and bright hallway lights. It was simultaneously exhilarating and terrifying.

We were leaving the first chapter of the post-transplant life and entering into our new unknown. Christopher, Jeff, and Tom had a naive belief that things were now going to be just rosy. I did not know everything to be entailed in this new life, but I knew many challenges and dangers still lay ahead. For the moment, however, I was going to revel in my son being alive and being with family. The sun was shining, the birds were singing, spring was turning into summer, and everything was absolutely right with the world.

Chapter 7

The New Normal

What might seem unbearable and unbelievable through the lens of a current life can become the "new normal." Many friends and acquaintances asked us how we could live through this. It all seemed so heroic from the outside. The simple truth was that we adjusted because we had no alternative. I screamed, cried, shook my fist at God, and then I just did it. This doesn't mean I liked it, but somehow it just became "normal." I longed to go back to how it was, but it never did.

The focus of our lives changed from whatever we thought was so worrisome and important—strategic work initiatives, getting As in school, and thinner thighs—to a different set of things we now knew were important—keeping Christopher alive and enjoying our family being together again. We had to adjust. We had no choice.

About one hundred thousand pills (give or take a few thousand) and hundreds of IV medications over a seven-year period was the new reality. These were not pills Christopher "should take." These were life-and-death, "must-take" pills. He took sixty pills a day for the first few months until his blood levels of antirejection medications got to the right level. Twenty-one horse pills that smelled like skunk were the main ones, and the rest of the pills counteracted their bad side effects. The day I came back with the box of medications and the pharmacist's instructions, I was in tears. This was a very complicated drug regimen for a chronically ill person, and it was heartbreaking to acknowledge this was now my son's life. My boys looked at me as if I was crazy. "They are just pills. What's the big deal?" Christopher said.

One prescription cost $2300 a month. Tom and I were unclear at this time whether our insurance would cover all these medications, and the financial burden looming was very worrisome.

The pills landed Christopher in the emergency room the first Christmas because the seasonal mandarin oranges he ate coupled with his potassium-hoarding medications caused a critically high potassium level.

The medication regimen was complicated and changed frequently, and I became the pharmacist who had to dispense them into small plastic bags, mark them by date, batch them by day, and rubber band them. Just making sure refills were called in and we were never without panicked me until I got the hang of it. It was a serious responsibility, and I worried about making a dangerous medication error. Thank God Christopher never refused to take his medication as I was warned some adolescent heart transplant patients did.

Schedules became unpredictable, and this bothered Tom (the "schedule guy") greatly. His work schedule gave him crucial grounding. He left for work promptly at 7:00 a.m. and walked in the door at 5:00 p.m. He took the same thirty-minute lunch break every day. During the first eighteen months, we couldn't know when we might have to drop everything and run up to the UW for a clinic visit or unexpected test. Luckily my job at this time was flexible, and I had an understanding boss and coworkers. Before Christopher's transplant I would feel absolutely torn if I had a child's event directly conflict with something important at work, and Tom would step up in a pinch and take the kids where they had to go. Almost losing my son rid me of this guilt and angst, and this was a huge step toward breaking my workaholic behavior. Kids absolutely came first and work second.

I had been constantly on call for work for years. Now my pager and cell phone were for Christopher first and work second. We had to plan outings and vacations around labs for blood draws and cell phone coverage so we could talk to Vic, the heart transplant coordinator at UW, if necessary. A scale, blood pressure cuff, thermometer, recording journal, and the box of pills became essentials whenever we traveled overnight. We took an IV pole, pump, and refrigerated medicine on our first post-transplant Christmas ski vacation in December 1997.

Tom and I hunkered down and did what we had to do during these years. Our relationship had always been solid and durable. We were not a dramatic, up-and-down couple. We hardly ever fought. I never worried our marriage wouldn't make it through the transplant. We had a close group of church friends who liked to sing, so we formed a four-couple group called Spiritwind. Our choir director was part of the group and picked out the most beautiful music for us to sing. We practiced every Friday night and then went out for wine and dinner together. It was a good activity we both thoroughly enjoyed. Spiritwind started shortly after Christopher's transplant and lasted for several years.

Constantly waiting for the other shoe to drop wore on us over the years. I had been a daily "wine with dinner" drinker, and now Tom took to doing the same. Alcohol was always a part of our boating vacations (celebratory drinks on sunny days), but now it all stepped up. I had partied way too much as a teenager and had secretly worried about my drinking getting out of control. My father had been an alcoholic but had several years of sobriety by the time Christopher got sick. I was afraid I might be following in my dad's footsteps but was even more petrified of not using alcohol as my all-purpose drug. It quelled anxiety like nothing else, and I couldn't imagine life without it.

We had two dogs during the transplant years, and while they were somewhat neglected, they were great sources of solace when we had home time. Tom particularly loved that no matter what kind of day he'd had, the dogs always greeted him like a rock star when he got home. Amber died of old age a few years after Christopher's transplant, and Shadow was killed running across the highway in 2001.

So Tom and Christopher decided I needed two new puppies for my fiftieth birthday. Without my knowledge they purchased two purebred black Labrador siblings and brought them home one day around my birthday. My first reaction was anything but gracious.

"*Are you absolutely out of your mind?*" I said to Tom. "We have a sick son, and now you bring two puppies into the mix. Are you totally crazy?"

I was so angry. My life was already reeling out of control, and puppies compounded that immensely. I hardly had time to shave my legs or pay the bills. I put my makeup on in the car on the way to work, and I raced home after stopping by the grocery store. I knew who would end up caring for these dogs—me.

Christopher loved the puppies and took such happiness from their cuddles. Mostly they were in the house piddling on the carpets despite our best efforts to housebreak them. We had a large fenced garden space where the dogs could play, and a kennel with a big dog house. Tom wanted them to stay in one or the other, and I hated having them cooped up. They would sit and look forlorn and I would feel guilty and let them out. We lived on five acres out in the country and our previous dogs had always roamed freely but stayed close to home. These puppies, however, kept running away and I would have to retrieve them again and again. I was my own worst enemy.

Tom got so mad at me. "They are *fine* in there. Leave them."

"Why have dogs if you are just going to lock them up in a kennel?" I would scream back.

I sat on the porch and sobbed because my life felt like a nightmare of responsibilities. They were crushing me, and I was powerless to do anything about it. Bottom line—the puppies were wonderful for Christopher and awful for the rest of us.

Magical thinking did not work, even in the "new normal." From the time of Christopher's transplant until his death, every time I saw the first star in the evening sky, I would say, "Star light, star bright, first star I see tonight. I wish I may, I wish I might, have the wish I wish tonight. I wish for health for Christopher." That pattern became so ingrained that it still comes immediately to mind ten years later.

Prayer in all forms did not save Christopher's life. We had prayer chains in hundreds of churches praying for all of us. I believe the prayer helped people feel as if they were helping us, and I am sure that good energy was sent to us, but I no longer pray for healing or a cure for any-one. I don't believe that is how God works. A decade after Christopher's death, I pray for strength, serenity, hope, courage, a sense of God's pres-ence, and acceptance. I don't believe God is going to save one child and let mine die.

Chapter 8

From Christopher's Heart—Journal Writing

Two years after his heart transplant, Christopher was a junior in high school, and he took a writing class taught by a wonderful teacher named Mr. Lester Krupp. Part of his assignment each week was to write seven pages on any topic in a journal. Little did we know this would be an emotional and highly cathartic outlet for Christopher. He did not share this journal, and it wasn't until after he died that we read it. This journal is an important part of his story.

Tomorrow I have to go up to the place I hate most and am most indebted to in the world—the University of Washington Medical Center. The conflict that goes on within me when I have to go to that place is extremely intense. One half of me loves the place because of my subconscious connection with the fact that if there is something wrong with me, going to the UW will make it better. The other side of me hates that place with the heat of a thousand suns because within those sterile, lifeless walls, the most painful, horrible experiences of my life have taken place. This clash within me spurs an extremely gut-wrenching mixture of apprehension and relief—a mix of happiness and dread. This mixture makes my senses reel.

—∞∞∞—

Depression. What is it? How can something stir up feelings of joy or jubilation, and the very next day the exact same stimuli can seem incredibly bland and very sad for no obvious reason at all? I try not to dig up the painful memories I have worked so hard to bury during the last few years, but I cannot stop them from resurfacing. Most times it is just a subtle smell or sound, and a wave of helplessness or horror drowns me. Even though it takes just a fraction of a second for everything to rush back, it might take days or even weeks to suppress the pain that comes without warning. Sometimes I think I am not strong enough to handle it, but as of yet, I am.

—∞∞∞—

I haven't had so much trouble the past two and a half years with anything as I am now. Most times I take these little health issues in stride. I roll with the punches, and it doesn't get me down. But I do see it as getting punched. Each instance is a punch. I can handle getting walloped every once in a while, but several successive blows are much more damaging. Right now I am completely and hopelessly behind in school, am fast approaching scholarship and application deadlines, and am in miserable health. I haven't been so down in years. If this continues much longer, I don't know if I will be able to get back up. The knockout blow is not far away, and if it comes to that, I don't know what I am going to do. I cry and cry and cry, and it doesn't get any better. I talk and try to remedy this growing pain, but my weakness doesn't go away. I hurt. I hurt like almost never before. Almost intolerable.

My object is a tiny Pabst ice beer can on a key chain. There is an interesting story behind this Pabst can. My mother went on a five-mile heart run on Sunday, October 10 (1998) where she received several little trinkets. This key chain was included. Later that night I was studying for my psychology test and playing with the little can in my mouth. I started having irregular heartbeats, so I stood up to go get a drink of water. Before I went ten steps, the world started going dark. I felt myself slump to my knees and then the floor. Everything went black. Things slowly began to lighten, and I awoke. My mother was over me screaming bloody murder. (I hate her twittiness.) I went to the hospital, and six weeks later I got the most worthless piece of shit contraption—a pacemaker. It totally ended my football career.

I sit here feeling guilty for being sad because of all the good things in my life that very few have. Yet I am *angry at everyone for not being wholly sympathetic of my situation. It's a great fucking enigma for some headshrinker to pick apart for one hundred dollars an hour. No man is an island, but I wish I was. I could be alone in my joys and sorrows without countless fake-ass people dragging me in the opposite direction than I am obviously intended to go. I could be entirely self-ish and sever all ties I had to the mainland. Let them have their preconceptions. They would never know the real me. I would bury it the way a pirate buries his booty—deep, deep somewhere and only to occasion-ally be brought out and cherished for short periods, lest I actually get enough confidence to show the real me to someone else. Though, this always ends in more pain. God knows I have had enough of that. Alas, I am open, honest, and straightforward to all those I meet. I keep my guard up about as well as a punching bag at Mike Tyson's gym. Try as I might I can't change who I am.*

In a weekly journal assignment where we are to write about what is on our minds, our troubles are bound to show up. Happiness is a simple emotion. When we are happy, we don't do deep soul-searching to sift out why we are happy. We just enjoy it. However, when we are sad, we find reasons to pick apart, ana-lyze, and work through the sadness. Thus, if there are deep, thoughtful things to be written, the overall tone might be negative. In other words, Mr. Krupp, I am not completely without hope. It just so happens I have a lot to deal with emotionally and physically, and one of the true outlets of my pain and anger is writing. My inspiration comes from pain and survival, so happiness is not a theme that appears in my writing much. In response to your comments, yes, a little reassurance now and again would be tremendously appreciated.

———∞———

In my current mood, I am afraid anything I'm going to write is going to have a decidedly dark tone. I can put on a smile and not let anyone know I'm unhappy inside, but in writing that seems so self-defeating since I write directly from my soul. Working through my problems by writing is very cathartic. What I write doesn't even have to be what I am down about. For instance, I can write about how I can't be dishonest in my writing.

I might have an inflated sense of my writing ability, but I consider my writing my "art." I am not an inherently talented person in painting or sculpture, but I find solace in my ability to express myself in words. I couldn't function if I couldn't express my deepest thoughts and feelings in some way. I certainly cannot sit down and just talk to a person about what is swirling around in my head, but I can spill out my complicated thoughts onto paper, and it is like a cranial pressure valve.

———∞———

I have a serious surplus of pent-up anger, and I need to vent it. I am going to use a lot of expletives, and I doubt it will make any sense, but bear with me.

I can't take it any longer—this goddamn intolerable condition that has decided I'm the prime recipient of pile upon pile of shit. Where will it end? The day I die will be a release from my shit-magnet existence. I've had every exam and procedure imaginable performed upon my body. It's to the point where my body is no longer part of me. It is a machine that allows my brain to get around. The hate! I have seething, burning hate for whatever or whoever is calling the shots up there and decided I was to be the one who got screwed and tortured through this zipper chest and fucking borrowed part that resides within me.

I ask the question every time the accursed pump beats. Why did this happen to me? What did I do to deserve this punishment? I wish I only knew so I could right this undoubtedly horrible transgression that slated me for such a fucked-up existence.

Fuck Fuck Fuck Fuck! No escape and no reprieve. I have become an entirely medical entity dependent on the ass-backward Western medical system and those pompous asshole doctors who think their new Jaguars are more important than the quality of life of their patients—simply "bodies" in their minds. Words cannot describe the complete distrust I have of those heartless bloodsuckers. They poke, prod, and dissect any way they can without any concern for the thoughts and feelings of this eighteen-year-old man who has a hard enough time getting by as it is.

I can still feel the needle entering my spine and prodding around. The detachment of my mind and body is extremely conducive to becoming a jaded, hateful person, and it hurts. Always with the jagged parts tearing and ripping my soul piece from piece, and the bleeding remainder is getting smaller and smaller. Soon I will become what I hate more than anything else—a husk. A drone. My soul will eventually just be a hard rock of nothing deep down inside me because it is easier to tolerate the physical without the emotional. I will be the perfect "patient."

I am struggling. I am trying. I am doing my best. The hand dealt to me for life is a random mess right now. I have had a lot of medications changed overnight, and the psychological as well as physical aspects of those changes are giving me a bad time. This change has not been as bad as some of the other medical journeys I have been on, but this is definitely not benign. These all-too-frequent shifts in my health have served to make me a very medically skeptical person. It has also made me a very resilient person, but all the resilience in the world still isn't enough all the time.

This change is reaffirming my experience. It brings the medical aspect of my life to the forefront, and it brings the feeling of unique loss into my mind again. I find myself remembering more than I would like to. My difference strangles me. I have a longing so deep and powerful to be a physically normal eighteen-year-old. It's a longing that can never be remedied. This normalcy can only be partially attained through a rather normal life—a life without constant reminders and constant jagged parts that cut and slice me and allow my mind to be infected with those hated, hurtful thoughts not of a sick child but a bygone fairy tale when I was the healthy one. When I wasn't the statistic. When I was a child.

I don't mean child literally, but then again in a sense I do. Freshman year I was an average fifteen-year-old. Then the hurtful time came, and I was torn from the womb. I was forced...no, dragged kicking and screaming away from my blindly optimistic, idealistic, fortunate happiness. I was dragged to a place where those things don't help, bad things do happen to good people, and people die. In a way I was rushed to the maturity level of an old dying man. As a defense mechanism, my mind took me to the end so I wouldn't die at the beginning caught in this void between childhood and adulthood. I want to do as I did as a child, but I am unable to capture that exuberance and love of youth. The jaggedness of the world is too evident and creates an impassible roadblock to reversing the process.

I can handle it. I am a strong person. The problems will not overwhelm me. I am stronger than anything that is thrown at me.

I hate the "oddity" stares the most. These looks make me feel as if I am a midway freak or bearded lady. All come to see the zipper-chest boy! These looks scream that I am "strange." They are sometimes mixed with compassion but bludgeon the resolve as time passes. My eighteen-inch freak flag (scar) is hidden behind clothes but is nevertheless seen through knowledge of personal hardship unappreciated.

Hard times are here. We are seeing once again how resilient Christopher Thomas Stewart can be. The people will know I have been gone from school, and they might very well know I have been sick. However, many will simply think, "Chris is always sick," and dismiss it without a second thought. Ailed by a virus synonymous with bitter old age but not. Experienced for the third time in tenderness and adding to the further hardening of a soul that wants to soften more than anything. There I go whining again. Where does the macho "Keep your problems to yourself" syndrome come from? Have we allowed society to bend our minds so far out of whack we cannot express our emotions as we would like, as is most cathartic, and as is healthy? Must we instead bottle them up, cork them off, set the time on the bomb, and let the pressure build until all functionality is lost—until we are left with huge amounts of things to vent, and when something sets us off, everything comes spilling out in a flood?

———∞———

Today I am happy. If I were bipolar, I would be in the manic swing of my cycle. Rather than my cycle being dependent upon the mix of chemicals in my brain, it is dependent upon my cycle of poor and good health. Just like a manic-depressive, when I have felt well for a period and fall ill, the blow of the sickness is crushing. There seems no bearing it and no way to get back up to recover, but after a long time of being sick, I get kind of numb to it all. These times are easier but also very scary. It gets easier the longer the duration, but in order to ease the hardship, I have to withdraw myself from the outside. I have to harden my soul to the blows and detach myself from my body. The reason this scares me so much is that when I'm in this state, I am not the Christopher Stewart my family and friends know and love. I become something different— a robot. Nearly every time I get in that state, it feels as though my soul does not want to come back out of its shell. Sometimes the duration of sickness is so long it seems my joy and happiness will never recover and return. It seems I will be condemned by my own pain to live a life of separation from the essence of my being. Just as it is extra painful to become ill, it is equally joyous upon recovery. It takes a few days to recover completely, and then bam! When I feel I have recovered fully, I suddenly regain my happiness and exuberance tenfold to what it was before the sickness. I revel in how good it feels to feel good. My energy level is about 150 percent of what it normally is, and I feel unstoppable. My parents dread these periods not because I am feeling better but because this reinforces my existing teenage invincibility, and I listen to nothing my parents tell me. Their advice is ignored entirely.

A month of two from now, I will have to psychologically face the pain from this shingles episode, and that will be difficult. While sick I have no energy to deal with it. I also don't want to deal with it when I feel well. I don't want it to be a total drag on my happiness. The point is that I feel a lot better and am completely and totally in love with life right now—at least for the moment.

—∞∞∞—

Well, my honeymoon with health has already ended. Can you see why I try to pack so many good feelings into my healthy periods? It is because those periods are few and far between. It wasn't even five days I felt good before I caught the common cold that is spreading like wildfire throughout the student body. It seems as if I live an existence where instead of health being the norm and sickness being the exception, the norm is sickness, and the exceptions are brief, sweet moments of health.

———— ∞ ————

Sleep. I require sleep. My head is swimming with phlegm, and I cannot think because my noggin is essentially a pressure cooker.

———— ∞ ————

Upon my last visit to the hospital, I was told I was as healthy as can be. I have a booming heart as strong as any athlete's, and every pressure measured inside my body is normal. Yet I don't feel well. There is nothing I love more than being told I am in great condition, yet when I don't feel well, that affirmation of my good health falls upon deaf ears. I just shut it out. It doesn't do any good to hear I am in the best of health when I'm not. Sometimes it seems as though the only thing I have to write about is my resentment of the medical system. Sooner or later I hope to get over that.

———— ∞ ————

At the end of the semester, Christopher's last journal entry was a letter to Mr. Krupp:

I want to thank you for being a great as well as understanding teacher. It seems as though you found your calling early in life and have done what you love as your career. You are lucky. Sit back and relax sometimes, and just enjoy being alive. Don't let the petty things (or even the important things) distract you. Just postpone everything for a second, and wallow in the glory of life. Those moments are few and far between, so enjoy them while you can. You never know when those glory days will end.

I'm not a worldly person, but there are certain life lessons I've learned. Love everything. Love your successes as well as your failures, love those you hate, and love those you love harder. Even disappointments are part of the human experience. Go home, hug your son, and kiss your wife. Be thankful for all that is taken for granted—down to the dust and bugs. In the absence of those little unimportant things, your life is changed. Only when taken away are they appreciated.

Accept all. Every person has at least something redeeming about him or her. There is no such thing as a not worthwhile meeting. There are no enemies—only friends you haven't yet met. Enjoy it while you can.

It's been nice knowing you. Have a nice life.
Chris

Here is a letter Christopher wrote to Tom and me in his senior year of high school:

I am sitting here attempting to gather my thoughts in a futile attempt to accurately express my emotions. I love you both more than words can describe, and my failure to show you this on a day-to-day basis tears away at my soul. I am sorry. I have been selfish in both words and deeds, and you have been the sole sufferers of my selfishness.

I have barricaded myself inside the thought that because it happened to me, it affected no one else. I overlooked the endless hours of vigilance you both were burdened by when watching over me. I overlooked the endless emotional support given to me, but most of all I forgot how selfless these deeds were, and I hate myself for it.

During the ordeal I believed I could be as strong as I needed to be to overcome my illness. I now realize my own strength was inconsequential. I had no strength. It came from you two and Jeff. It was not my strength. It was our strength that allowed me to continue, and this has gone on for the past three years. You have given and given with no return. When you say I am an inspiration, that is a lie. I have done what is necessary to survive. You are the inspiration. You have had the strength to pick me up repeatedly, forgive my failures, and lead your own lives.

You two are the foundation upon which my world is built. I would be nothing without you. Without the love and support I have been given, I would have ended it long ago. I am serious about that. Sometimes my experience grabs a hold of me so tightly it feels as though death would be an appropriate exit. However, you are the constant in my life—the eternal shoulder to cry on. The fucked-up existence I lead is only made bearable by the ever-present love of you both. I am awed you can love such a flawed person with such intensity and keep me going through what I have been faced with.

I only hope that someday I can be as inspiring to you as you have been to me time and time again.

Mom, Dad, I am alive today because of you two, and I pray to God I never forget it. I love you both so much!

Christopher

———

Here is my letter back to him:

Dear Christopher,

Happy third heart birthday. What a trite expression to describe such a gut-wrenching experience. I am sorry we don't do justice to your anniversaries. I don't think we can.

We lived alongside you during your ordeal, but we aren't you. We have lived every day with you since, but we haven't lived your life. We have our own demons in the night about what happened, but we can't know yours.

As parents there is nothing we would like to do more than take this burden away from you and put it on ourselves, but we can't.

Know we love you and never want to disappoint you. We want to support you however we can. Help us by telling us how.

Love,
Mom

Chapter 9

The Forsaken One

The summer after Christopher's heart transplant, Jeff jokingly called himself "the forsaken one." We were all in Seattle while Jeff was living at home in Olympia. He was by himself much of the time. He got up at 4:00 a.m., made his own lunch, worked all day, washed his own clothes, and rattled around the house alone. He was nineteen at the time, had been away at college for a year, and was totally capable of handling his own affairs, but it was lonely for him. All the attention since early April had been focused on his younger brother's health crisis. Jeff had been like a third parent in May. He took his turns in the rotation of staying at the hospital, but he had to be in Olympia in the summer to earn money for college.

Tom had found Jeff a job with a dirt and utilities contractor for the summer. Jeff was working with the elderly owner of this small-town company who was also an itinerant preacher on the side. He was an angry, crotchety old fellow who spent the day alternating between yelling and preaching at Jeff. It was definitely not ideal, but Jeff was making good money for school, so he bit his tongue and worked his tail off.

Jeff felt quite guilty about his brother getting so sick on his "watch," even though he realized the illness was lurking under the surface and waiting to erupt. What-ifs plagued him. What if Christopher had dropped dead when Jeff was forcing him to run up the stairs or for the Frisbee? It made him ruminate over the many comments he had made about his "lazy-ass brother." Jeff had a strong work ethic, while

Christopher had always been the less robust one. Christopher was the one with the right-sided weakness and the anxiety. He was the one who always got hurt, hated most of the Boy Scout outings, and didn't carry his share of the load with chores.

From the beginning of his life, Jeffrey was an independent kid who had the stability of his beloved maternal great-grandmother as his primary babysitter for the first three years. He was at the one hundredth percentile for height and weight, and he looked a full year older than he was all through toddlerhood. He had straight brown hair, sparkly brown eyes, an impish smile, and an even temperament. He was constantly in motion. He was not a sleeper, a lover, or a hugger. Jeff walked at ten months and slept as little as possible. The only time I could get a cuddly Jeffrey was right before bed or when he was sick.

As Jeff grew he maintained his independence. He was a well-liked, strong student and a good citizen in his classrooms. He had a sense of empathy for kids who were different and got picked on, and he often took them under his wing. He played soccer and football. He was never the best on the team, but he was a good team player, and all his teammates liked him. He also loved to ski, and we always had a winter ski trip as a family.

Jeff was motivated to work, and at thirteen he went away to Scout camp for a good part of the summer as a counselor in training. It didn't bother him a bit to be away from home. He didn't get paid that first year, but the next two years he did. From thirteen on he always had a summer job, and in high school he worked part-time at a sporting goods store. He played football in high school and had a coach he adored and a team he bonded with, even though their win–loss record was abysmal.

The first semester of high school, Jeffrey really applied himself scholastically, as he was very nervous about the new, bigger school. He got a 4.0, and from that time on he quit working so hard. He never got bad grades, but if he had applied himself, he could have gotten a great GPA and gone to whatever college he wanted. Now as a thirty-six-year-old computer engineer, he does wish he had worked harder in high school and college, but nothing I tried would motivate him at the time. I now tell him this is the challenge he can conquer with his own children! Jeff and

I always got along well, but we did fight over two main themes during his high school years—his grades and my workaholism. It drove me crazy he was so smart and applied himself so marginally. He hated that I worked way too many hours and was always late getting home. We finally made a pact that I wouldn't harass him about his grades, and he would lay off about my work hours.

Jeff's first real love affair occurred when he was a sophomore, and it ended badly. It hurt too much to be emotionally open and trusting, and he tucked his emotions out of reach—even to himself. He became more cynical. Whether it was his size (6'4"), his brains, or his appearance, he always had access to the most popular kids. Many years later, however, he admits he never felt connected to them. Although happier with the "computer nerds", he always felt it was expected he be one of the "in" crowd, and he was. He was universally liked and appeared very comfortable in any social situation. He was nominated as senior class speaker at graduation because both his teachers and peers respected him.

Jeff was part of the high school party crowd and always liked organizing and working at parties. He says now it gave him something to do, and he didn't have to interact as much with all the kids. Years after high school, Jeff told his dad and me about huge parties he would hold at our house when we were gone for the weekend. He and his buddies would remove all the furniture and breakables (Jeff made a diagram) and well over one hundred kids would show up to party. The next day they would shampoo the carpets, pick up all the cigarette butts, and replace the furniture exactly as it was. We would come home and have no idea anything went on. Jeff rarely got caught doing anything he wasn't supposed to do. He was that kind of a kid.

Jeff applied to one college—WSU. It was a low bar and nearly guaranteed admission. He had a great time his freshman year until Christopher got sick. Returning his sophomore year, Jeff had lost the lightness and innocence of his freshman college experience. At that time he didn't even know how to name his emotions. He had a hard time taking anything academic very seriously. He had spent too much time in the ICU with his brother on the verge of death to worry much over an assignment. There was no one in his peer group who could relate to his experiences. Jeff went to parties, but he had trouble engaging in lighthearted college banter. Life and death issues in his family made everyday college life seem trivial.

Jeff admits seventeen years later that he was angry at his brother about his life and the family's lives being turned upside down. He knew it wasn't his brother's fault, but it continued to fit a pattern of Christopher's weaker, sicklier place in the family. When asked why Jeff never shared this with his dad or me, he said, "There wasn't much capacity in the system to handle it." As the mom, I should have been more insightful, but Jeff hid his emotions well, and I never even suspected his anger.

At the end of the post-transplant summer, Jeff felt sort of lost. He got an MIP (minor in possession of alcohol) that landed him in jail in Eastern Washington for twenty-four hours. The judge told him if he got into any other trouble, it would be thirty days in jail. Jeff then proceeded to get his first speeding ticket as he continued to a big weekend concert in Eastern Washington.

Christopher, Tom, and I were on our boat vacation in South Puget Sound during this week, and Jeff was supposed to join us on the weekend. We couldn't connect with him due to poor cell phone reception. When he finally reached us by phone, our rock of an older son was very shaken. All the troubles of the previous week (his MIP, speeding ticket, and time in jail) came spilling out as he told us about the "worst week of his life." We told him to get to the boat, and we would take care of him. He was worried we would be furious, but we weren't at all. We felt badly for him and about his troubles, and we were ready to help him any way we could. This was another case of big life troubles putting the smaller ones into perspective.

Returning to college the next fall, he got another MIP on campus. He was scared to death two MIPs would land him in jail for up to thirty days, so he immediately quit drinking for the entire school year.

His plans for engineering were nearly derailed after his brother's heart transplant with the thought he might want to be a cardiologist. He kept his engineering classes but started taking premed courses for electives. He and his grades suffered under this heavy load, life with his girlfriend was tumultuous, and Jeff didn't know what was wrong. He was having nightmares and not sleeping well. He felt listless and unfocused.

I encouraged him to go see a counselor at the free school health center, and he did. Although he didn't talk much about it, it seemed to help him greatly. He could at least name some of his emotions and understand how Christopher's brush with death was impacting his life.

By his senior year, Jeff had dropped the premed classes and was finishing out his degree in computer engineering. Christopher was also attending WSU by now. After the heart transplant, our sons had really bonded, and their overlapping year at college together made them even closer.

Christopher had a very successful freshman year, and I give most of the credit to his big brother. Whenever Christopher got anxious or needed support, Jeff picked him up from the dorm and brought him to his house to stay until he felt patched up again. They hung out together, and it was like a home away from home for both of them. The school was across Washington and a good six-hour drive from Olympia. Tom and I felt much more comfortable about Christopher knowing Jeff was keeping an eye out for him.

Chapter 10

Nothing Is as Important as Being Together

Christopher's classmates voted him to be the senior class speaker at his high school graduation in 2000. I don't think he was chosen because of his adversities but rather because his classmates liked and respected him. Tom and I were there and very proud of him. We were especially proud that he did not talk directly about his heart transplant and its many challenges. Rather we felt his wisdom shone through along with plenty of "dude."

Last Sunday I was on my way back across the state with my brother, Jeff. We had just spent the weekend at WSU. (Go Cougs!) The car radio went haywire, so we had no tunes for the whole six-hour drive. I am surprised we kept our sanity.

Among the topics we discussed on our marathon journey was what I would say as class speaker on this very prestigious day. We talked about what I would compare life to. We tried everything from Teva sandals to tequila shots, and over the course of our discussion, I was reaffirmed in something that has kept me going these last few years.

I realized then that the topic of our discussion was equally as unimportant as this speech itself. What was most important is that we were together. We were spending time with those we loved. You see, I have personally faced a fair amount of adversity in my youth, and through it all there has been only one constant in my life—the love and support of my friends and family. That is the thing that is important above all else.

I don't want to lessen our accomplishments in any way, but a diploma is only a means to an end—a stepping-stone for a better job or to get into college. The real worth of our high school experiences lies in the collection of seemingly inconsequential memories we have all shared. Although they didn't get us letter grades, they shaped us and defined us as individuals.

So my advice to you, the class of 2000, is to look around you. See all the people who have shared in your glories, failures, successes, and defeats. Love and cherish them as long and as much as possible while you still have the time, because after today nothing will ever be the same.

I want to give thanks to Debbie and Rhonda, our fantastic cafeteria workers without whom we would have gone hungry all those long school days. Thanks to all the teachers for not only putting up with us but doing it every day. Thanks to my family—Mom, Dad, and Jeff. I wouldn't be here without you. Thanks to the Piscopo household for the festivities last night, and last but not least, thanks to all the bros. I wouldn't have had any fun without you.

I wish all of you success in your ventures, love in your relationships, and peace in your hearts. Thank you.

Chapter 11

Lazy Masquerading as Sick?

During his high school years, Christopher talked with me about his anxiety issues concerning the heart transplant. He and I spent many evenings sitting on his bed in his room. He was tearful and worried about the future, and I was trying my best to reassure him. He rarely shared with anyone else his worries about a very short life. He was thankfully able to put them on paper in his journaling. At the end of high school he wrote:

> I am coming to a point in my life where very soon I will leave the nest and be able to fly. I will depart from the places and people I have known through my entire young life and strike out on my own. Most of the faces I have seen day in, day out for the last twelve years of my schooling, I will never see again. The loss of the comfort zone will be refreshing and difficult at the same time. It will be refreshing because a fair number of people I see daily I don't particularly like. I don't hate them either, but coming from a school district where everyone in the senior class has been at the same school since sixth grade means the group stagnates. It will be difficult, though, because even though I am bored with it, it's a comfortable boredom. The rut of high school is a nice, safe way to spend four

years of life. I get up, eat, go to school, come home, eat, and go to bed. It is a time when very few things in life matter greatly—when one can be irresponsible and carefree and not have the real world swoop in to ruin everything.

As a youngster I always thought I would know my path by the time I was college-bound. Over the past few years, I have come to learn that most people never find what they are searching for and have to settle on paths not quite meant for them. Even more recently it has occurred to me I might be one of that unfortunate majority. I really hate the thought I've faced the hardships I have only to end up doing something I don't enjoy for the rest of my adult life. I would like to think some higher power had grand things in mind when I was put here, and I would accomplish something in my time here.

I have only a few short years to live life to the fullest of my ability, but how am I to know the way without a road map? I would love to be able to force this thought out of my head and just take this crazy ride as it comes, but the uncertainty is too much to bear. I am quietly and anxiously taking a voyage of self-discovery in everyday life.

Christopher's journaling during his freshman year at WSU was more raw and worried.

February 26, 2001: This is the first journal I have had the balls to write in going on one and a half years. My pot-hazed mind isn't quite on the level. Ironically my hand is already beginning to cramp just as I begin to give myself my one and best outlet.

I don't want to write this as a memoir of some great testament to my dysfunction or longing for a better life. I write because it keeps certain jagged edges and personal demons from cutting and biting me—especially when the springtime comes. It's not spring yet, but spring is no longer a season for me. It is much more a period of emotional turmoil. The happy, pretty time of blooming flowers and burbling babies is associated in my mind with such astounding pain and suffering. Maybe that is not so ironic, considering I was reborn in a way. I was given a chance to bloom and flourish in my own unique way—a way I still wish I had never been privy to.

I am trying to deal with the reality of my near death four years ago coupled with what my head has come up with to compensate for all the screaming and burning of what would have happened. The fact I live because someone else died is pretty fucking real. One very healthy, young person died so that I—a smart kid but a pothead—could live. I will not have that good soul's intent wasted upon a worthless cause. I will, I must create a better good. I am alive, and gratitude is owed for that, but I cannot even address the hurt that resides within me.

March 6, 2001: What am I doing? I'm not going to live to a ripe old age or anything close to it, so why would I waste five years or more in academia? I have had enough drunken college stupidity in my first year at WSU, and I already know who I am. So what's the point? I love to learn, but by the time I reach the work-force, I'll be a fraction away from dead. I've always wanted and been expected to attend college, but just when I get here, I have the profound realization that 4 years of college might take all the life that I will have. Is this what I really want?

Christopher had a successful freshman year at WSU, but after his brother, Jeff, graduated, he had no interest in being that far away from home. He applied and was accepted at The Evergreen State College in our hometown of Olympia, and he moved into a college apartment with six other guys for his sophomore year. Now he lived only twenty minutes from home. I talked to him on the phone regularly, and he would drop by from time to time, but mostly he was independent of us.

Being back in Olympia had both benefits and distractions for Christopher. His high school friends were making little of their lives at this point and partying a lot. He fell back into that familiar groove. Alcohol and pot had become mainstays to keep away his "death demons"—his anxiety about his shortened life. This added extra guilt, as he was not treating his body as well as he should after the great gift of the heart.

He made it through fall quarter of his sophomore year at Evergreen, and then the wheels started coming off. He needed to find a job for the summer, but no matter how much I prodded him, he wouldn't take any action. His dad was thoroughly disgusted with him, and their relationship was tense. Jeff would call Christopher out on it. "Get off your lazy ass, and find a job! I have been working since I was thirteen. You are nineteen and have never had a serious job. That's ridiculous."

It seemed that just when we would be ready to push him, Christopher would get sick. Tom and Jeff quit believing him when he said he didn't feel well. Jeff coined the expression, "Are you lazy masquerading as sick, or sick masquerading as lazy?" This was our dilemma. It was very hard to tell the difference. Christopher did have some legitimate health hiccups, and when these occurred I would tell Tom and Jeff to back off and let him get well.

I was witness to more than one episode where he got very drunk. We had always had a close, trusting relationship, but now it was strained. The end of the line for me was catching Christopher in a great big lie. A weekend that he desperately needed to study and catch up at school he had gone to Victoria, Canada for a partying weekend with his high school friends. He had sworn to me that he had not gone and then I found a hotel room key in his pants pocket as I threw them into the wash. When we came face-to-face, I started shaking and crying. "Christopher," I said, "I don't know what is happening to you. I don't know who you are anymore, and I am really scared for you."

Christopher dissolved into tears, and we hugged each other and cried for a long time. He admitted he was a mess. His schoolwork was in shambles, and his attendance and attention had been horrible. Some of the attendance issues were from illnesses, but he had "milked it to the max," and his professors weren't having it anymore. He was smoking way too much pot, so his memory and motivation were in the toilet. He was ashamed of himself and totally miserable. As we settled down and talked, he made a plan.

Christopher did not want to go to counseling but agreed he would meet once a week with his and our good friend Pastor David Nelson. He wanted to move home, stop smoking pot, stay away from his high school friends, get his shit together (as he said) with his studies, and look for a part-time job. I reminded him he was an Eagle Scout who had completed his project—a wildly successful blood drive at our church—when he was not feeling well after the heart transplant. If he could do that, he could pull himself together now.

Pastor David (as we called him) had cemented his relationship with Christopher a year after his heart transplant. Tom and I were hosting a brunch at our church for family and friends to thank them for their incredible support that year. At this time Christopher was dealing with a serious virus and on IV medication twice a day. Both Jeff and Christopher thought the open invitation brunch was a stupid idea. They thought it was as if we were trying to "celebrate" the one-year anniversary of the heart transplant, and they did *not* want to be there.

Pastor David understood all that, so he made Christopher a special present and wrapped it up in a nice box. David asked Christopher to open it at home, but he was too curious, so he went into the church kitchen and opened it up. It was a leather glove filled with clay that was fashioned to give the finger. The intent to Christopher was clear. Give God the finger for what happened; God can take it. Christopher *loved* it. He and Jeff thought it was the coolest thing that our pastor could capture Christopher's anger at the world with this creative present.

Christopher contacted Pastor David and they started having lunch once a week. David recalls that their weekly get-togethers were as good for him as for Christopher. A few months before, David had a heart attack and required open-heart surgery. While they were X-raying him after the surgery, the doctors found a large abdominal aortic aneurysm. This was a weak area in the most important artery in the body. Many people die when these rupture, and most people don't know they have them. So only two and a half weeks after open-heart surgery, David had to have another major surgery to fix the abdominal aneurysm. The recovery from two major procedures in such a short time was difficult.

David was trying to put a positive spin on his health problems by telling Christopher he was lucky the doctors found the aneurysm. He was grateful they were able to fix it because he could have died from it. Christopher stopped him right there. "There is a time to be grateful and call yourself lucky, but it's not until you take time to grieve and be angry. It sucks to have two major surgeries in less than two months. It sucks to have a heart attack, so admit that. Take the time you need to be angry and sad and depressed about it. Don't let people tell you how lucky you are. That makes me crazy! After you get all that out, *then* you can be grateful."

Pastor David to this day says this was an important life lesson Christopher taught him.

Over the winter and into spring, Christopher kept his part of the bargain, and it was clear he was feeling better about himself. He had a new sense of control and purpose. He had found a new interest in international politics—especially in the Middle East—and his class evaluations started reflecting good effort. He found a part-time job in the dietary department of the hospital where I worked, so he had some spending money of his own for the first time ever. He was more clear-headed and peaceful than he had been for a very long time. Even the onset of spring did not cause him to despair as it usually did.

Christopher was now six years post-heart transplant in May 2003. At his annual checkup he was told he was the picture of a good long-term heart transplant patient. His heart was strong, the coronary vessels were large and clear, and they said this heart would last him a long time. It was great news to get in the spring—a time when the ghosts of the terrible spring of 1997 and the cardiomyopathy usually haunted him.

In the spring of 2003, everyone in the family was actually doing well. I had received a promotion to hospital administration a few years before and was finally getting the hang of the job. I had decided I needed to do something about my drinking and had begun to go to alcohol recovery meetings. Jeffrey was working in Seattle, making good money, and falling totally in love with his new girlfriend, Christina. Tom was back in his routine of work and his favorite pastime of working on the boat on weekends. The Stewart family was in its best shape in a long time.

Chapter 12

Now We Get to Deal with Cancer

Christopher got back to the hospital room after dark. At first he was comfortably groggy, but then he started experiencing extreme pain at his surgical site. "The anesthesiologist put in an epidural, so there should not be any pain at the surgical site," the nurse told us.

An epidural is a catheter that goes into the spine and delivers pain medication directly to a certain area. In Christopher's case, it was to the lower abdomen. The benefit is that the whole body and brain are not fogged up with pain medication. The downside is that the epidural can easily dislodge, and then it stops working. Christopher was very direct in his request for more pain relief. "I don't think the epidural is working. This thing is starting to hurt like hell. I need something for the pain."

"We will contact the anesthesiologist and see what he says."

That was the first delay. It was Saturday, and there was only one anesthesiologist on call, and he was tied up. Christopher's pain was escalating, and he looked increasingly alarmed. The nurse came back into the room and adjusted the epidural rate. "This should help in a few minutes," she said.

Christopher's pain was getting quickly out of control, though. "I need something IV until this kicks in. This is unbearable."

The nurse put on the intercom so she could speak to the desk. "Page the doctor again. Tell him the epidural doesn't appear to be working."

Minutes seemed like hours. Christopher was now writhing and swearing. The nurse couldn't do anything without the doctor's order, and she was waiting for him to answer his page. I was dying inside for my son but also knew it wasn't the nurse's fault. I said something to Christopher like, "Yelling at the nurse won't help."

He looked at me incredulously and spit out his words with such anger. "Really, Mom? I am supposed to be quiet and polite and not make a scene because you are a nurse and know everyone here and don't want me to embarrass you? Jesus Christ," he went on. "I have just been cut open and had a big chunk of my intestines cut out, and the goddamned epidural isn't working, and I am not supposed to shout? Fuck you! I need something for the pain. *Now!*" By now sweat was pouring off his face, and his pupils were dilated and wild like a caged animal's.

What was the reason for all this pain? Christopher's second medical tsunami had hit. We were all reeling. Christopher had a portion of his bowel surgically resected to remove a large cancerous tumor in his colon the day before Father's Day 2003. The immunosuppressive medication he had to take to keep him from rejecting his heart had effectively muted his immune system for six years and left him wide-open to cancer. His luck had begun to run out, and we were all still in shock to think of our heart transplant survivor dealing with another possibly fatal illness.

The anesthesiologist walked into the room, looked over the epidural, turned it off, and gave a verbal order to the nurse for some morphine IV push. "It must have dislodged when they transferred you to the bed," he said.

I would like to think there was a sincere apology, but I don't remember one.

The first medication barely took the edge off, but thank God, it did help a bit. Christopher was big and had built up a tolerance to narcotics over his many years of medical procedures. They soon had a PCA (patient-controlled analgesia) pump in the room, and Christopher could push the button and give himself his own medication.

Memories of Christopher's terrible pacemaker experience eighteen months after the heart transplant welled up, and it made me sad and angry that despite all the good people who work in health care, a patient could suffer so terribly due to breakdowns in the system. This episode was not as life-threatening as some others, but the sudden lack of pain medication made his vital signs unstable. The far worse injury was the instant loss of trust and sense of anxiety it caused Christopher. It takes a lot of positive experiences to make up for one traumatic episode such as this one.

Tom, Jeff, and I all settled down in the room. We were very shaken and irritable. "God, Mom," Jeff said, "why do you always have to be so polite? You should be standing up for Christopher—not explaining why the nurse can't get something done!"

He was extremely angry at me, and I was shaken up. Watching my child in such terror and pain was indescribable. "Jeff, if it sounded as if I was making excuses, I am sorry. No one wanted Christopher to get pain relief faster than me. I just know the rules and how the system works. Screaming at nurses when they are powerless to order a medication makes the whole situation that much more out of control."

I later apologized to Christopher. "Christopher, if it felt as if I wasn't standing up for you, I am truly sorry," I said with exhausted tears running down my cheeks.

Christopher didn't acknowledge my apology. He was still too freaked out by what had transpired. We were back in medical hell. The day before (the Friday before Father's Day) I had received a call that my dad had been taken to the hospital with stroke-like symptoms. By the time I got to the ER, my dad's symptoms had improved, but they were going to admit him and watch him. Christopher tried to call me a few times while I was with my father, but reception was very bad in the emergency department, and I kept missing his calls. I finally stepped outside to call him back. I was sure he was trying to find out about Grandpa Larry because they were very close. When I heard Christopher's voice, I said, "Hi, honey. Did you call to see how Grandpa is doing?"

"No, Mom," he said in a tight, strained voice. I could tell he was very frightened. "I have been calling because I went to the bathroom and blood filled the toilet bowl."

"What?" I replied. Christopher had been complaining of some inter-mittent, severe stomach pains, but I thought it was his normal spring "stress stomach." I figured it would be better after finals. "Oh my God!"

"Mom, I am so scared. It was a lot of blood. It has happened twice, and I am at work, and I don't know what to do."

"Tell your supervisor you are having a medical emergency, and you need to go the ER right now. I will be there in thirty minutes."

I raced back into my father's room with my heart pounding, and I told my parents about Christopher. After six years of a heart transplant, it wasn't totally a shock Christopher was having a medical issue, but it had actually been quite a while since something serious had come up. Mom and Dad told me to go and let them know the situation when I got there. I kissed them both good-bye and headed to the parking lot to see how fast I could get from the Tacoma ER to the Olympia ER.

I found Christopher scared and angry. "Why does this shit always have to happen to me? Goddamn it!"

His hospital uniform—khaki pants and a purple shirt—was crum-pled in a ball under the gurney he was lying on.

"What do we know? Anything yet?" I asked as I threw my stuff in a chair and went over to give Christopher a kiss and a hug.

"The ER doc came in and looked me over. They ordered some labs and a CT scan. I have to drink this shitty contrast. They say it is berry flavored, but it tastes like chalk. They are going to admit me I think."

"How many times did you have bloody stool?" I asked. I was trying to get my bearings.

"Four times, and God it freaked me out when I looked in the toilet bowl."

"God, honey, now I feel horrible I pooh-poohed your stomach pain. I thought it was the same stress stomach you have had the past several springs with finals."

"I know, Mom, but I did tell you it was killing me."

Guilt started to consume me. This time it was with a vengeance, and I could feel the familiar flush of panic it always caused. Why hadn't I told him to call his gastroenterologist? Life just went so fast. We were all so busy, and Christopher had been so healthy. I had been lulled into more complacency than usual.

Christopher's lab tests showed he had lost quite a bit of blood. He didn't need a transfusion but was definitely going to be admitted. He went off to the X-ray department for his CT after he had swallowed all the chalky contrast. He was back soon, and then he was moved up to the surgical unit.

By the time we got to the room, it was late Friday afternoon, and Tom had joined us. We called Jeff and left a message on his phone. He called back and talked to his brother. Christopher told him to hold off coming down to Olympia until we knew what we were dealing with. Christopher was to have nothing to eat or drink until they figured out what was going on, and he was hungry. He hadn't eaten all day. Christopher was a big boy—over 6'4" and about 260 pounds. He rarely missed a meal, so he was not happy with this situation.

One of the most revered of the general surgeons at our local hospital, Dr. Chris Griffith, came into the room. I greeted him and introduced my husband and then Christopher.

"Hi, Christopher. Do you go by Christopher or Chris?" asked Dr. Griffith.

"Chris," said Christopher.

"OK then. So tell me about your stomach, Chris. Have you been having pain?"

"Yes. I have been having this pain in my stomach for a month or so."

"Can you show me where?" the doctor asked.

I cringed when I saw where he was pointing. Christopher's pain had always been around the stomach area, but this time he was pointing much further down on his abdomen and to the right side. I hadn't asked him to show me exactly where the pain was, and he hadn't said it was in a different spot. The nurse in me was once again panicking. *Shit! What have I done?* My worst fear was always that I would miss something crucial, and now I had. Even though the oncologist later assured me the outcome wouldn't have changed if the cancer was caught earlier, this haunts me to this day.

"Chris, your CT scan is abnormal and suggests something in your intestine. We can't tell exactly what it is with just the CT, so you need to not eat or drink anything tonight. Tomorrow morning the gastroenterologist on call will do a colonoscopy to see if we can visualize it. Once we know what we are dealing with, then we can make a plan. Do you have any questions?"

"Do you mean there is a growth or something?" Christopher asked. This was exactly what I was thinking.

"Let's not get ahead of ourselves. I'd rather not speculate. You try to get some sleep tonight, and we will know a whole lot more after the colon procedure."

After the doctor left, we worried to ourselves and settled in for the evening. Tom stayed until dark and then headed home. I stayed in the room. Christopher had his colonoscopy midmorning the next day. Shortly after he returned to his room, Dr. Griffith appeared. He was dressed in surgical garb. "Chris, we are taking you to surgery. There is a large tumor in the wall of your ascending colon, and we need to get that out right away. I have added you onto the surgery schedule for today. Since it is the weekend, I can't tell you exactly when we will get to you but probably midafternoon. The nurses will get you ready for surgery, and I will be back later to have you sign an informed consent for a bowel resection surgery."

Preparations started immediately, for which I was grateful. Once we heard the word "tumor," our minds started shouting about cancer, and getting the tumor out was paramount. It was the day before Father's Day.

"Happy Father's Day to me," Tom said darkly.

Christopher pounded his fist on the bed. "Son of a bitch!" Tears erupted from his eyes, and he wiped them angrily with the back of his hand. "Goddamnit! Everything has been going so well. School is going well, I have a job, I have a car, and I am not being a pothead. I have my life straightened out, and things are good at school. Now *this*! So fucking unfair!" He groaned and began weeping big racking sobs.

Soon we were all huddled together and trying to console him. We didn't know exactly what was coming, but a large tumor meant cancer, and our thoughts led down a very dark path.

Christopher went to surgery late Saturday afternoon, and they told us it would be three to four hours. It was a beautiful June day—an anomaly in Pacific Northwest weather.

Tom said, "They have our cell phone numbers. Let's get out of here for a bit. The Perkins are home. They want us to come over, and I want a gin and tonic."

The Perkins lived about ten minutes from the hospital. Hugs and sympathy greeted us, and we all went out onto their deck to sit in the sun. *Twenty-two days of sobriety be damned,* I thought on their deck. *There is no way I can quit drinking now.* I accepted a glass of chardonnay. Alcohol was my go-to drug for major stress, and I wasn't going to be—I couldn't be—without it that day. I promised myself I would go back to "those meetings" when my life settled back down.

After the surgery and the nightmare with the lack of pain medication, Christopher settled in for the night, and I stayed with him on a horribly uncomfortable cot next to his bed. The next morning Dr. Griffith told us the bad news. "There was a large tumor in the intestine that eroded the wall. That was why Christopher had so much blood in his stool. We took a large piece of intestine, and I also took several lymph nodes for the pathologist to test. It looks as if it could be malignant, but we won't know for sure until the pathologists give us their report. That can take three to four days."

"What happens next?" Tom said. He suddenly looked small and hollow-eyed.

"I will leave a message for an oncologist to see him," Dr. Griffith said.

I stood to shake his hand, but Dr. Griffith grabbed me and hugged me.

"Thank you so much for taking Christopher to surgery as soon as possible," I said. "Having that tumor out already makes us all feel so much better."

He shook Tom's and Jeff's hands. "You are welcome," he said. "I will write post-op orders and will see Chris tomorrow morning. If they need anything for Christopher, they will page me."

Monday morning Tom went to work. I called in to my work and told them what had happened. I told them I would be taking at least the entire week off. Word got out to the prayer chain of our church, and supportive calls and cards started immediately. Pastor David visited Christopher every day in the hospital.

By Wednesday we hadn't heard anything from pathology. Christopher's primary care physician in Olympia was a great friend, a coworker, and an infection control specialist. He was used to taking care of immunosuppressed patients, as he had many HIV patients. Christopher's medical challenges were more from immunosuppression than directly from his transplanted heart, which had been working great.

I asked this doctor if there was anything on the chart from pathology, and as a favor to me, he said he would look and come to the room if there was. He was going out of his way to do this for us. As he walked into Christopher's room that afternoon, he looked shaky and ashen. Father of two boys himself, he read that pathology report and thought "death sentence." True to his word, though, he came to tell us what he knew. "Hi, Chris," he said as he approached the bed. "Um...the pathology report is here, and it isn't good news. The tumor is adenocarcinoma, and many of the surrounding lymph nodes were positive."

"So what's the treatment?" Christopher said. The doctor's grave demeanor alarmed him.

"The oncologist will talk to you about this, but my understanding is that with this many positive lymph nodes with this type of cancer, there are very limited treatment options."

Tears started running down Christopher's face as he took this in. "Shit!" he said. "I have gone through all this, and now I am going to die of *cancer*? Not from my heart but from *cancer*? I can't accept this."

Christopher's doctor stood in the awkward silence and looked as if he was going to faint right along with us. I felt sorry for him. He had done this as a friend, and in retrospect that was not fair to either Christopher or him. He said, "I am so sorry, Chris," and he quietly left the room.

Christopher kicked Tom and me out of the room. "I need some space. I just want Jeff here. Go take a walk or something."

Tom and I walked down the back steps and bolted out the side door of the hospital to a grassy section on a sloping lawn. We sat down on the lawn and sobbed. It was not unusual for me to cry, but for Tom to cry was almost unheard of. Sobs racked him for several moments.

Christopher had lived through so many life-threatening events. He had become bulletproof in our minds, and we had started to believe he was immune to death. We couldn't believe that he now had an untreatable cancer.

When Tom dried his eyes, he said, "OK. That's it. Those are the last tears I am crying. We are going to do everything in our power to fight this. I am not going to just roll over and let my son die. No way. No! Call the UW. Tell them about this path report. Maybe Olympia doesn't have anything to offer Christopher, but I bet the UW does."

I did call, and after consultation with the UW, Christopher's diagnosis was changed to beta cell non-Hodgkin's lymphoma. We received this news and actually celebrated. Such are the highs and lows of living on the medical edge. It was a scary, aggressive cancer, but compared to the sure death sentence of adenocarcinoma, it was at least treatable with a standardized chemotherapy regimen. Christopher, we were told, had a fighting chance. Christopher grabbed onto this shred of hope with both hands and regained his fighting attitude.

He went home from the hospital on the fifth day. He needed some time to heal from the surgery before the chemotherapy started. Six weeks was the normal amount of time to recuperate. Christopher required six rounds of chemotherapy, and this began four weeks after his surgery. Because of his heart transplant and the fact that one of the chemotherapeutic agents, Adriamycin, is hard on the heart, he was admitted to University Hospital in Seattle for the first round. The chemotherapy started right about the Fourth of July.

Christopher had a huge mixture of emotions during that hospitalization. On the one hand, he was glad to get the treatment going, and he had trust in UW Hospital. However, the Fourth of July was his favorite holiday, and instead of cruising around Lake St. Clair with his best friends in the party barge, it was spent in a hospital. Across the hall from his room, I could see a magnificent Lake Union fireworks display. I rushed back into Christopher's room and got him out of bed to see it. He walked out with his IV pole and stood watching for a minute. I could see the tears starting to roll down his face as he turned back to his room. "I can't watch this, Mom. It's too depressing."

Christopher and his heart handled the first chemotherapy session uneventfully, so he was discharged home to continue treatment as an outpatient in Olympia. We needed to make a plan for Christopher's care, as his treatment would continue once every twenty-one days for six rounds. He would need to get to the doctor and the outpatient infusion center, and Tom and I had to figure out our work schedules.

Luckily Christopher's best friend, Tyler, did not have a summer job. We hired him to stay with Christopher during the day and take him to any appointments. I went back to work part-time. I had no idea how I was going to do all my work in twenty hours a week when my normal workweek was about sixty hours. Goddamnit. How was a mother supposed to handle this? Once again I was very angry I had to struggle with this question. Tom resumed his full-time work. Jeff was working in Seattle, and he came down when he could on weekends.

After his first round of chemotherapy, Christopher was very nauseated, and his appetite was gone. Eating had not been a problem before the therapy. Christopher asked for medical marijuana, and the oncologist agreed and faxed a referral. These were the very early days of medical marijuana, and it was not yet common. Off we went, mother and son, to the medical marijuana store, Green Cross.

I stopped at an ATM and asked Christopher how much money I should take out. I had never smoked pot as a teenager. Booze had been my drug of choice, but I knew a lid of pot was ten dollars back in my day.

"You'd better get two hundred dollars, Mom," Christopher said.

"What?" I choked out. "You're kidding. It costs that much?"

"Well, the good stuff does," Christopher said rather indignantly.

I laughed out loud as I got the money. I was glad we had the money to spend, and I thought, *I can't believe I am taking my son to buy pot, and I'm happily paying for it!*

The time came for Christopher to go to the "pharmacy," and I wasn't asked to join him. I waited in the car. It was a gloriously sunny day, and I was enjoying sitting and reading. Christopher was gone so long I began to get worried, but he finally came around the building with a little bag in his hand and a big Cheshire cat smile on his face. He had tested out the "medicine" in the pharmacy and was definitely feeling the positive effects.

He got in the car. I looked at that little bag and said, "That is it? That little bag? Can I see it?"

He pulled out two pill bottle containers. There were little green clumps that looked like tiny broccoli heads with some leaves attached to the stems. It didn't look anything like the stuff I had seen years ago.

"Mom, in those days it was all just leaves and stems and low quality. This is very high quality."

"So, did you buy the best?" I asked, but I already knew the answer. Christopher always had champagne taste.

"Of course!" he said. "For God's sakes, I have *cancer.* I need the best," he said in a mocking tone.

As we drove back home, we both relaxed, and I enjoyed Christopher's high as much as he did. If this drug was going to make him less anxious, less nauseated, and have a better appetite, then he could smoke away.

Tyler started coming every day to be with Christopher. This gave me much peace of mind. Both were total slobs, and I kept the house stocked with easily prepared, microwavable food. (Thank you, Costco!) Tyler drove Christopher to his doctor appointments. The rest of the time they watched TV, played video games, and smoked pot. Who wouldn't like doing that for ten dollars an hour?

Christopher's six rounds of chemo started in July and continued through November of 2003. When I turned fifty that August, the puppies arrived in our lives. Tyler and Christopher loved the puppies but let them run wild around the house, and they piddled everywhere. We had to cut out the carpet by both doors in the family room because they were so urine-soaked. Nearly every night Tom was shampooing the carpets. Schedules and clean carpets meant a small semblance of control over our lives to Tom.

During Christopher's second round of chemotherapy, he developed an infection and had to go back in the hospital. It was a Sunday midday. I went to church and then to the hospital. Tom and Christopher were watching a movie in the hospital room as I walked in. It was the horror suspense thriller *Misery* staring Kathy Bates and James Caan. Everything was getting to me that day—my work, Christopher's cancer, and now his infection.

I came in as Kathy Bates tied James Caan's legs to a crossbar and used a sledgehammer to break his ankles. I snapped and started sobbing and screaming. "I can't believe you can watch such horrible stuff!" I yelled at them. I could hardly breathe and felt as if I was choking for air. "Our life is so horrible right now—our real life right here and right now. Then you watch something so horrible happening to another human being. It is so dark and awful. Isn't our life bad enough? I can't stand it!"

They looked at me with a mixture of anger and astonishment. I was the peacekeeper in the family—the one who numbed her emotions with wine so she didn't overreact—and I was screaming at them. I grabbed my purse, stormed out of the room, and ran down the back stairs. Since I had been a nursing supervisor at this hospital, I knew every nook and cranny. I knew how to get out of there fast.

As I was walking out of the lobby, I ran into the Perkins who were coming to see us. I was hardly coherent as I sat with them for several minutes and tried to explain myself. I told them to go see Christopher. I was going home to try to get rid of these emotions.

The whole drive home I wailed, keened, screamed at God, said every bad word I had ever learned, and told God I *hated* him. I could hardly see to drive, and I was speeding. I got out of the car at home, and I felt totally out of control. I had to do something to get rid of this anger. I threw my backpack on the ground repeatedly, but that didn't help. I went around the back of the house with a bat and started swinging at an old woodpile. That really hurt my hands and didn't relieve the tension. I tried slamming the bat into some old tires. I couldn't get the relief I needed. I was breathing hard and walking around like a wild creature.

I went in the house. I was usually not a hard liquor drinker, but I grabbed the first bottle I could find, held my nose, and chugged. I felt as if I was going to burst if I didn't release this energy. I paced up and down the hall. I was breathing heavily as if I had just run a sprint. Then the liquor started to take effect, and I collapsed in a sobbing heap. I feared for my own sanity at that point.

How could I have done something so crass? I hadn't chugged hard liquor straight out of the bottle since I was in seventh grade. I poured a large glass of wine and drank that quickly. The temper tantrum finally eased. I prayed to God to forgive me for everything I had said, and I thought over the previous hour or two. I didn't want God to think I hated him. I needed him to save my son and also help me survive.

Around that time Christopher started using the expression "shit magnet." He called himself that, and he called our life that. Always the optimist I usually looked for the brighter side of life, but even I was having more and more trouble finding the silver lining in anything.

I hated feeling this way. My optimism had always worked for me, and it scared me to think the world was indeed as unpredictable as my family had recently experienced it. During this period of our lives, I had my rose-colored glasses handed to me in a shit sandwich, and it shook me to my core.

Somehow we managed to get through the six rounds of chemotherapy, and Christopher had a follow-up CT scan in early December that was clean. Tyler had taken Christopher to the appointment, and when they came home, it was indeed a celebration with drinks all around. Christopher was jubilant but exhausted. The six months of medical poison had physically taken its toll. He was bald, anemic-looking, and out of shape but in remission.

My son now had a large abdominal scar along with the one that ran down the middle of his chest. He also had his pacemaker scar and the Medi-Port scar. Sometimes I couldn't stand to see these marks on my son and be reminded of all he had gone through. On the one hand, I felt as if my comeback kid had dodged another huge bullet, and he was indestructible. Underneath my jubilation was the knowledge this was a very aggressive cancer. I could only hope and pray it was gone.

Chapter 13

How Not to Celebrate in Barbados

For Christmas Jeffrey suggested a real adventure. His girlfriend Christina's stepfather, Tim, was on assignment in Barbados. Tim worked for the Department of State, and his job was overseeing security during the construction of embassy buildings. Christina and her mom, Bea, were going to Barbados for Christmas, and Tim had offered to rent us a condo in the complex where he lived while on assignment. Jeff told us Tim would be our tour guide, and it would be a great celebration after the six months of hell we had gone through. Jeff's ulterior motive was that he really wanted to be with Christina over Christmas.

I was ready for an adventure. We had never done anything like this before. Our family vacations were always skiing in the winter and boating in the summer—usually very familiar and controlled surroundings. Tom was leery of this Barbados trip. He thought it was bad luck to celebrate so soon, and the thought of being in another country spooked him. It was a lot of money, and he needed much encouragement to finally agree. Because of his reluctance, he did not lift a finger to make any arrangements and was very quick to point out anything that didn't go perfectly in the trip's planning or execution. This made it all the more burdensome for me, but I was determined we were going to do this and have fun together. Jeff, the most traveled of our family, thought we were being overly fretful about the details. He told us, "It's not hard to travel. You buy the plane tickets and *go!*"

Finally the day came. At 10:00 p.m. on Christmas Eve, we boarded the first of three flights to Barbados. Sitting in the airport and having drinks on Christmas Eve seemed odd but also exhilarating and sort of cosmopolitan. By the time we arrived at our destination, we were no longer exhilarated but tired, crumpled, and hot. The heat hit us like a steam bath, and we were wringing wet as we stood in a long line in the customs area of the Barbados airport.

I was carrying luggage for Christopher and Tom and felt like a pack mule. To keep the peace, I figured I would take care of all that while Tom sniped at me about any inconvenience. "This is a third world country, you know," I sniped back at him and rolled my eyes.

Tim, Christina, and Bea were a very international family. Bea and Christina were originally from Belgium. They had lived all over the world on Tim's assignments and must have quietly chuckled about the hayseeds from Washington State whose entire travel experience up to this point was a handful of ski resorts, the Puget Sound, and two trips to Disneyland.

This was our first meeting with Christina's parents. As they picked us up from the airport, Bea saw me struggling with all the luggage and looked askance at both Tom and Christopher. I made a face that said, "Don't ask!" We loaded everything in their van, and they took us to a beautiful condo right on the water. The water was the most amazing blue, and the sandy beach was a lovely light tan with palm trees and colorful flowers. *Yes*, I thought. *This is going to be great!*

We immediately jumped into beach attire, went for a swim, and then celebrated with some of the island's famous Cockspur Rum Punch. All four Stewarts swimming in the warm Caribbean water and then sharing a cocktail seemed like the beginning of a perfect and much needed vacation. I thought I had died and gone to heaven. The rum punch tasted fantastic, and it was strong. After one drink I was lit. Tim had received a very large ham as a Christmas present, and had split it in two and put half in the refrigerator of the condo he rented for our family. "You never know what you might find or *not* find at the supermarkets here,", Tim told us. "This might be the most American thing you eat all week!"

We had dinner that night up in Tim's condo, and then we walked down the street to explore. Like many places with hot climates, Barbados comes alive at night when the sun is down and it is a bit cooler. There were many restaurants, bars, and shops. There was also live tropical music. It was all very exotic and intoxicating. Walking at midnight in light clothes with a warm breeze was something we got to do maybe once or twice a summer, so this was a real treat.

The next morning Tom and I woke in our lovely sunlit room. From our bed we could watch and hear the ocean. We were all a bit slow off the mark from the partying the night before, and we had to get to the store to stock up on groceries. First Tim gave us a short tour around the small village. Driving was on the left, roads were very narrow, and there were people and traffic everywhere. I was very glad Tim drove. Renting a car, driving on the wrong side of the road, and navigating would have put Tom over the edge.

The grocery store was broken-down and dirty. Its smells were unusual and strong. Since we got to the store on Boxing Day (the day after Christmas), the stores were stripped of most fresh food and all dairy. I was supposed to cook that night for both families, and I had no idea what to prepare. There was no meat except for chicken feet and pigs knuckles. There were no vegetables I recognized or fruit. Everything looked small, limp, and beat-up. I had never been out of the country, and I didn't know what to do without a fully stocked grocery store within an easy drive. I don't know what I cobbled together for dinner, but it was not memorable.

The next night we were all going to a fish fry in an adjacent town. I had already had a couple of rum punches and was feeling no pain as I flew down the spiral steps from the third to the first floor of our condo. I did not see the last step and came down hard on the side of my foot. I am no small girl, and the speed I was going made the impact significant. The pain sent me sprawling onto the gravel. I scraped my shin and really hurt my ankle. I was embarrassed and mad at myself because I didn't want to inconvenience anyone or admit that alcohol probably played a part in this accident. I ended up back in the condo with my leg elevated and iced, and the rest went to the fish fry.

One afternoon the entire troop went completely across the island to a tourist site where they advertised sea anemones. The Puget Sound has big, colorful sea anemones, so we all imagined a lush tropical paradise of anemones. We climbed down a long set of rickety stairs through a sea cave, and at the bottom was *one* tiny, beat-up sea anemone. We thought this was hysterical! Another day we went to a monkey preserve and wondered where they all were, but we did see something that looked like a cross between a rabbit and a deer.

Jeff was obviously happy to be around Christina, but Christopher felt a bit like a fifth wheel. The first night he went out on his own he met up with some island locals I think he was looking for some pot because he couldn't bring any with him on the plane. They scammed him. He thought the whole Bob Marley Rasta movement was cool and was bewildered when this scam occurred.

Christopher didn't say he felt poorly, but he didn't look very well. He would break out in a sweat frequently, but being so hot that didn't seem unusual. He skipped a few outings and chose instead to stay at the condo. I was sad about this because I so wanted "normal" family vacation time. Although we had many good times, there was a subtle undercurrent of fear and unease.

There was a liquor store next to our condo, and Tom insisted on some gin and tonic. Rum was extremely cheap on the island, but gin went for fifty dollars a fifth. Gin was what Tom wanted, though, so we bought him some. It was something familiar, and that made him feel a little more in control and a little more normal. We were all desperate for normalcy, but in a foreign land, in stifling heat, drinking too much, and with people we didn't know well, we were all a little lost. I started to think this "once in a lifetime" vacation was really a stupid idea.

Bea, Christina's mom, had a PhD in psychology, and she would try to engage Christopher in some meaningful dialogue about his illness and its effects on him. I, of course, wanted everyone to get along, but from the first time he met Bea, Christopher felt she was trying to fix him, and he resented these attempts. He would be almost rude in his nonresponses. He did *not* want to go there with her, and he didn't. He was on vacation and trying to forget all the life-threatening issues.

We were literally thousands of miles away from home for almost two weeks, and international calling was very hard, so we didn't communicate with anyone in Olympia. When we arrived home, we found out there had been a prolonged freeze after a big snowstorm. On the drive home, the freeway was a lumpy, icy, rutted mess, and the side streets were even worse. We hadn't anticipated any unusual weather and had done no additional planning for an extended freeze. I have pictures of us rolling our suitcases from the van to the house through more than a couple feet of snow. When no water came out of the tap, we knew we had frozen pipes. We put the heat lamp in the pump house, plugged in the heat tape in the garage, and turned the heat up in the house. As the house started thawing out, we could hear water gushing. Tom and Jeff had to go under the house in the freezing cold to fix the pipe. Luckily only one broke.

The snow and broken pipe were a fitting end to this vacation. We were all so excited to have fun, but it just didn't come off. Tom was characteristically wary most of the time, Christopher never felt great, we all drank too much, and I spent too much time trying to make sure everyone was happy. Instead of a truly restful, soul-rejuvenating time, the whole trip was expensive and stressful.

Chapter 14

From Joy to Grief in Forty-Eight Hours

After that vacation we were all glad to be home and back in our normal routines. It was January 2004, and Jeff went back to work in Seattle. Christopher started school again at Evergreen for winter quarter. He was so happy to be going back to school after time away for his cancer treatments. He was planning to live at home for a while until he got back into the routine and could find a place and some roommates. He bought his books and started studying as if his life depended on it. He once again started reading everything he could get his hands on about the Middle East, and it felt good to him to have substantive things to focus on that did not include cancer.

Grandpa Roger, Tom's father, was going to marry Kathryn. Roger and Kathryn had been together for six years. The wedding was planned for January 18—two weeks after Roger's eightieth birthday. Tom rented a room and arranged the catering for a reception after the ceremony. It would be "family only." Sharon, Tom's oldest sister, was a Superior Court judge, and she performed the ceremony in her black robe. It was so much fun seeing Tom's siblings and their children. All the kids were together and grown up—in their late teens and early twenties.

All the men wore suits, and Kathryn wore a lovely ivory dress and matching pumps. Tom was the happiest I had seen him in years. He loved Kathryn very much and was so happy his father had found another wonderful woman to share his life with. Caring for Betty Jean, Tom's mother, through her Alzheimer's had taken a big toll on Roger, and all the kids were glad to see a spring in his step and a smile on his face. Kathryn was quite the character. She had a great sense of humor and a way of enjoying life that brought Roger out of the doldrums. Betty had been a teetotaler and had gotten really irritated with Roger when he would stop by his mother's house on the way home from work to have a couple drinks with her. Kathryn, on the other hand, enjoyed her cocktails very much, so she and Roger would relax with drinks before dinner nearly every night. This fit with our lifestyle, and we enjoyed watching Roger's normally serious demeanor lighten up.

On the ride up to the ceremony in the car, Christopher remarked that he had a pain in his right side under his ribs. Knowing Christopher's dietary habits, I told him his gall bladder might be acting up. He was very young for this kind of problem, but for some reason transplant patients have a higher than usual incidence of gall bladder disease. I told him if it continued he should go to the doctor and get it checked out.

After the ceremony we all went out to a special party room in a well-known Tacoma restaurant. The gathering was warm and joyous, and Tom was smiling ear to ear. The food was excellent Italian. My parents came as well as many old friends, so it was a wedding celebration and a reunion. Tom looked very handsome in his suit with his silver hair, and I felt very close to him that night.

That Monday Tom and I went back to work. Christopher called in the early afternoon to tell me the pain in his side was killing him, and when he called the doctor, he was told to go to the ER to get it checked out. I remember ducking my head out of my office and telling Shannon, my executive assistant, that I thought Christopher was having a gall bladder attack. I told her he was in the ER at St. Peter, and I needed to take off. I made some crack about Christopher liking gravy on his fried potatoes and not being really surprised. I told her I would fill her in later in the afternoon, and I would probably be back late afternoon to finish up.

I arrived at the ER and was taken back to Christopher's room. He was miserable. He had not had anything for the pain and was waiting for the doctor to come in. I kissed and hugged him and told him they would probably get a gall bladder ultrasound to see if that was his problem. I was convinced it was nothing more than that.

The doctor asked Christopher about his pain. "Well, I have had it for about a week. Sometimes it hurts much more than other times. At first it came and went, but right now it is there pretty much all the time," he said. He was pointing to his side as he talked.

I told the doctor that Christopher, despite my harping, ate a really high-fat diet, and I was thinking this pain was from his gall bladder.

"It's in the right place for a gall bladder. Let me examine Chris, and then we will have a look on our portable ultrasound." He did his exam, and when he pushed on the area where the pain was, Christopher really winced. "Boy, that is tender, isn't it?" the doctor said. "I will be right back with the ultrasound."

He covered Christopher's abdomen with the conducting gel and started looking. "Now here is the gall bladder," he said and looked at the ultrasound image that neither Christopher nor I could decipher. "It actually looks fine. Not distended or abnormally large." He kept probing and watching, and then his brow furrowed. "There is something here under the gall bladder. A mass of some sort."

With this my body reacted the way it had reacted so many time before. I was light-headed and sick to my stomach. My pulse was racing, and I had an icy feeling in my extremities. How could I have been in such denial that I was sure this was something as benign as a gall bladder? This was a cancer recurrence. I looked at Christopher, and he was taking in this information. There were no tears, screams, or profanities. He just lay there taking it in.

The doctor looked at his watch and then at me. "Chris's oncologist is just down the street, right?" he said.

"Yes," I answered.

"It is four forty-five. I am going to call over to his office to see if you can go over there before they close for the day." He left the room, and I grabbed my cell phone. I told Christopher I had to call work to tell them I wouldn't be back. I called Tom.

When I walked back in the room, Christopher quietly said, "Mom, I am so sorry for what this is going to put our family through again."

There was no, "Shit. I am so scared for myself." Christopher was not always so selfless, but in that moment he was totally in that space.

Tom had a particularly visceral reaction to the news. The Stewart men were not comfortable with extreme emotion. Going from the heights of joy at his father's wedding to the grief of the cancer recurrence nearly unraveled Tom. It was as if he thought his joy had caused this tragedy to occur. I didn't understand it at the time, but I think the first real unhinging of our marriage began then.

They gave Christopher something for the pain, he quickly got dressed, and we drove down the road to the oncology office. By then it was after hours. The doctor looked flushed and grim and said, "We will have to restart chemo as soon as possible. I also need to discuss this at Tumor Board and the UW to decide our best course of action."

A PET scan was ordered, and Christopher went in early the next week to have it. The results were beyond sobering. PET scans show where there are fast-growing cells (cancer cells being the fastest growing of all), and Christopher's abdomen lit up like a Christmas tree. The oncologist did not describe it in these terms, but the look in his eyes revealed that the results were indeed grave. He told us there would be two rounds of chemotherapy in Olympia. Then we would take Christopher to Seattle for a stem cell transplant.

Christopher was anxious to start treatment again. "We are going to get right up into this bitch's face and give it all we have got. I am not going to survive a heart transplant so I can die from cancer. No way!"

When Jeffrey heard about the cancer recurrence, he went to his boss and asked him (or maybe told him) he needed to telecommute from Olympia two or more days a week so he could be close to his brother. Our neighbor, a Comcast installer, made sure we had the highest-speed Internet—a feat in our rural location in 2004. We set up a desk, and Jeff plugged in. Jeff relayed a story of being on a work call and hearing Christopher yell to him from the family room, "Jeff, come smoke some weed with me!" As the total slob of the family, Jeff dropped clothes everywhere and left wet towels on the bathroom floor and toothpaste residue in the bathroom sink. It was *wonderful* to have him home!

The chemotherapy was indeed harsh and knocked Christopher for a loop. During one of his many emergency department visits during that period, an IV nurse was having a really difficult time accessing his Medi-Port. That meant she had to repeatedly stick a big needle into Christopher's chest. I could see Christopher get more anxious and angry as this poor nurse kept trying. Finally Christopher just erupted. He took off his glasses, flung them across the room, and shouted, "Goddamnit! Get away from me! Get someone in here who can do it right!"

His chest was heaving, and his eyes were wild. He was sweating and more upset than I had ever seen him. The nurse and I were practically in tears. I couldn't stand watching that panic in Christopher's eyes and knowing he was the victim of a bunch of fallible human beings in the health care system. Another nurse was called, and Christopher got some Ativan. This helped to calm him down. The next nurse got it in the first stick, and I thanked God profusely.

How many more times could I watch my son in panic, pain, or terrible fear? We were trapped in medical hell. It was a nightmare we couldn't control where little went smoothly or the way we wanted it to. All roads going forward were tortuous and painful. How were we going to get through this? I dreaded the future but also couldn't stand the present. *God,* I prayed, *I can only get through this with you holding me.*

Dr. John Harlan, my sister's friend and head of hematology at Harborview, became our liaison between Olympia and the Seattle Cancer Care Alliance (SCCA). It was comforting knowing someone so knowledgeable was overseeing Christopher's care. In order for Christopher to get the stem cell transplant, we had to move to Seattle for four months. This meant we had to find someone to take care of our dogs and make arrangements at work. We basically had to stop our lives. This was not an easy task when both Tom and I had very busy full-time jobs. Another requirement for a stem cell transplant was a dedicated twenty-four-hour-a-day caregiver. Given I was a nurse (and because I wanted to), I was assigned that role.

A replacement had to be found for me at the hospital. My position at the time was assistant administrator for patient care services at Providence Centralia, a 110-bed hospital, and I was in charge of all patient-related functions. Luckily the person who had retired from this position when I was hired agreed to come back for as long as needed. Thank you, God!

Everywhere I went at work I got hugs and reassurance. One ER physician wrote "Peace and TLC" on a prescription slip. As my leave began, I felt a huge burden lifting. For the past six months, I had felt torn between the demands at work and home, and I had failed at both. Now I could focus all my energy on doing the thing I wanted most—taking care of Christopher and my family.

Christopher's friends learned of his cancer recurrence, and they all started spending more time at our house. With Jeff home and all these other people in and out, the food budget skyrocketed. I was again cooking for a bunch of young people and loving it. In the midst of this crisis, the house became alive again in many ways. Even when the septic tank overflowed, the bathtub filled up with poop and Roto-Rooter had to come and save us, it did not dampen our spirits.

Tom and I had many friends wanting to take us out to dinner, wish us well, and send us off to Seattle. Four nights in a row, Tom and I ate out with friends. Alcohol flowed freely each night, and I found myself drunk four nights in a row. With my safety net of work removed and my extreme emotions, I was wide-open for the worst alcohol abuse since my adolescence. Each night I would start with a plan for how I wouldn't drink too much, and I would wake up sometime in the early morning hours with the gut-wrenching realization I had lost control again. The physical distress from too much alcohol along with the guilt and remorse culminated after those four days with the shakes (for the first time in my life) and a determination I had to get back to an alcohol recovery program.

That Monday morning I found a recovery meeting at noon at my own church. I sneaked in and prayed I wouldn't see anyone I knew. I was so scared and beaten down. I'd had terrible hangovers in my day but never with hands shaking as they were that morning. A friendly woman introduced herself as Toni and asked if I was new. I told her I had gone to a few meetings the previous spring. With tears streaming down my face, I told her I was really scared of what was happening to me. I admitted that once I started drinking, I couldn't stop. She took both my hands in hers and told me I was safe here, and there was hope. She suggested I go to a meeting every day. She took my phone number and asked if she could call me the next day. I told her that would be wonderful.

I don't remember much of what was said in that meeting, but I felt a sense of calm afterward. It was kind of like the feeling after a long, cathartic cry. I knew I had to get a handle on my drinking, or I was going to be useless to Christopher. I committed to getting to meetings as often as I could.

As I kept going to the twelve-step meetings, and with the burden of my job removed, I began to experience a sense of peace and centeredness like I had never known. I would later realize it was a spiritual awakening, but at the time all I knew was that my craving for alcohol stopped, the chattering voices in my head stopped, and I felt a deep peace in the middle of the toughest time in my life. My mind stopped living in the future where fear and dread resided and in the past where all regrets lay. All the taunting, awful voices that had driven me to "succeed" my entire adult life came to a halt, and for the first time in my life, I knew what the expression "the peace that passes all understanding" meant.

I started reading a little recovery meditation book my father had given me. It had helped him get sober many years before. Each day had a little reflection about alcoholism, something spiritual, and a prayer. The spiritual reflection for each day was such an indescribable gift. The words seemed to fly off the page and right into my heart: "Wear life as a loose garment," "All in God's world is fundamentally well," "Loosen your hold on Earth, its cares, and its worries," "Live in the world, and yet live apart with God," and more. Everything was pointing to the fact there was so much more in God's world than the suffering on the earthly plane. I felt profoundly that I was not a human being having a spiritual experience but a spiritual being having a human experience. Whether Christopher lived or died, we were in God's hands, and he was taking care of us. For the first time since the start of this nightmare, I knew that whatever came, I could get through it.

Christopher and I were moving into the Pete Gross House in Seattle—an apartment building dedicated to patients undergoing treatment at the SCCA. Jeff was moving back to his duplex in the Ballard neighborhood. It was about a twenty-minute drive from SCCA, and Tom was going to work part-time and split his weeks between Seattle and home. He had to hold onto some of his normal routine, or he couldn't function. We each had our own needs and quirks, and we tried to tolerate that in each other.

Tom said he didn't want to bother me with all his medical questions about Christopher. He asked if I minded if he consulted a friend of ours, a nurse practitioner, about medical stuff. I told him that was fine with me. I was annoyed at him for not moving up to Seattle full-time with us. At this point I didn't care what he did. I did not yet know, however, how far apart we had really grown.

Christopher was ready and even anxious to get to Seattle and get on with the lifesaving stem cell transplant. Tom was sighing a lot and looked haggard. His son was critically ill *again*, and it felt so unjust. His worldview (work hard and be a good person, and life will treat you fairly) was shattering, and he was grasping for a lifeline of some sort. Jeff was glad this next treatment was closer to his home and job, but he was afraid of what was to come. He was having stress-related symptoms such as light-headedness, an upset stomach, and trouble sleeping. I knew a stem cell transplant was Christopher's only chance, but I didn't know if I could bear to watch the suffering I knew it would cause.

The only redeeming factor for me was that Christopher was over eighteen and made his own medical decisions. If he had been underage, and I'd had to make the decision for him to undergo this treatment, it would have been infinitely harder to watch him go through it. I had a Seattle alcohol recovery meeting schedule and hoped to get to meetings to hold onto the peace and serenity I had begun to find underlying all the craziness. I was fervently praying I could keep my sobriety and inner peace through this last-chance treatment for my youngest son.

Chapter 15

Visiting Hours Are Between Never... and Go Away

Christopher was very young to have to deal with the hand life had dealt him. Some of his coping mechanisms were healthy and others were not so much. My son had very little control over his medical situation, but who was in his hospital room was his decision. It was his domain. As with the heart transplant, he made it clear he did not intend to spend time in the hospital without a family member. He usually was not keen on anyone but immediate family, especially when he was not feeling well. That meant every minute of the day and night, Tom, Jeff, or I was there. Christopher was not hospitable if he didn't want a person there. For the rest of the world, visiting hours were between never... and go away.

Christopher tolerated short visits from grandparents, certain aunts and uncles, and close family friends, but mostly our nuclear family was his circle of support. This was breached once during the pre–heart transplant ICU stay by an overzealous church worker who came and stayed for hours because she once had a teenage daughter in the ICU and felt she could relate. We did not know her very well, and she did not seem to catch Christopher's glares or my subtle suggestions she leave. I got an earful from Christopher after her intrusion.

Christopher did not even want his friends to visit when he was really sick. He knew if he called them, the first question would be, "How are you doing?" He just didn't want to go there if he was feeling sick. Whenever Christopher was feeling better, he asked for his phone and called a friend. He was also hesitant to make plans for friends to come visit, though, because his treatment schedule frequently changed at a moment's notice. More than one visit from a friend had had to be shortened due to unforeseen medical circumstances. He would then get angry and disappointed.

Anger was one of Christopher's initial coping mechanisms after the heart transplant. Terry, one of his best friends, said that when Christopher first got back to high school after the heart transplant, he was angry and kind of hard. He had little compassion for what was going on with anyone else, and his lack of sympathy and outbursts of anger alienated a lot of kids. "He did not suffer fools lightly," Terry remarked.

About a year or so after the transplant, the anger dissipated. Terry wasn't sure what had happened, but Christopher became more open to everything and everybody than he had ever been. "I am not going to give this anger any more energy," Christopher said one day. One of his journal entries pertains to this:

> When I was sick in the hospital, a part of me got really hard. The only way I could cope was to harden myself to other people's problems and issues and consider them unimportant in comparison to my own. For nearly a year, I was hardened to other people, and everything they were going through had no room on my plate.
>
> As my health improved and the difficulties of being a heart recipient decreased, I slowly realized I had enjoyed having all the friends I alienated. It wasn't that they were different; it was that I was different.
>
> However, it is much more difficult to regain friends than to get them in the first place. I have lost and found my compassion.

He realized that the anger and resentment were eating him up and keeping him from the very thing he craved most—doing normal teenage activities with normal teenage friends. He was able to regain the friends he had lost.

Jeff's description of Christopher's recipe for medical emergencies was laugh out loud funny to me: four Percocets, two bong hits, and an Xbox. Keeping anxiety under control was critical, and Christopher had plenty of reasons to be anxious. During his cancer he had very legitimate reasons for taking Ativan, Percocet, and marijuana. He had tumors pressing on organs, painful procedures, and horrible nausea and vomiting as side effects of chemotherapy. That said he never tried to limit his relief. The air in our family room at home was blue from marijuana smoke much of the time during his first six rounds of chemotherapy. When we got to Seattle, he could no longer smoke marijuana due to the potential for lung infection, so it was ordered in a pill form called Marinol. We also made marijuana chocolate chip cookies that we kept in the freezer. Christopher used these liberally and shared them with his brother and friends.

Pain medication needed to be taken at times, but I knew how addicting the narcotics were. I had seen them destroy many lives. I was always wary and cautioned Christopher about using them too liberally. He didn't listen, and I am now glad he didn't and took what he needed to lighten his mood and take care of his pain.

Music was always important to Christopher but even more so during his illness. He asked for a new device called an iPod before his stem cell transplant, and he filled it full of music when we first got to Seattle. Angry hip-hop seemed to be his favorite. He could unload a lot of negative emotions by putting on his sunglasses, putting up his sweatshirt hood, putting in his earbuds, and shutting out the world.

Christopher could get lost in video games and spent hours playing. This took his mind off the cancer. Xbox Live was brand-new. He could play with his friends over the Internet, and he loved it. He could also play with people from all over the world and frequently did.

He got relief from being with his friends, hanging out, and watching TV or movies. Christopher and Jeff watched movies, *South Park*, or *Chappelle's Show* frequently and laughed themselves sick. I noted that things that would normally be considered mildly funny became hysterical in these emotionally charged times. It took his mind off being sick and back to just being a normal guy.

Christopher had always had kids at the house before he got sick, and he was a generous host. The Pepsi and snacks flew out of our kitchen as his friends gathered around the television. Hanging around, watching TV, and joking with his friends in the hospital or Pete Gross House helped him feel as if he was healthy and home.

Christopher needed physical reassurance. He was a big bear of a guy, and he loved hugs. Christopher hugged his friends openly, fully, and unabashedly—not a common thing for a young man to do. During his hospital stays, the bed's side rails had to be up because they held all the controls. This made it very difficult for Christopher to get much physical contact, so he would make it clear when he needed some. "I need a hug," he'd say.

Christopher used humor to cope and had ways of finding joy amid all the medical madness. While he was living in the ICU waiting for the heart transplant, one of the nurses copied jokes off the Internet for him. This was a treat as the internet was quite new and these jokes a novelty. Jeff and Christopher would practically roll on the floor laughing at some of them. Jeff said he had never laughed harder than one night in the ICU with Christopher reading something called the Darwin Awards. The Darwin Awards commemorate "those who improve our gene pool by removing themselves from it"—usually by doing something really stupid. The boys also had a hoot driving a red remote control car all over the ICU the night of Jeff's birthday. That surprised a lot of nurses and patients.

During Christopher's time at Evergreen after the heart transplant and before the cancer, he and his roomies found a universal key to the pay washers and dryers used at campus housing. They made the rounds once a week and took some of the money out of these lockboxes to fund a weekly Thursday evening party. Christopher said they were like Robin Hood—taking from the rich and giving to the poor (themselves). Apparently this went on for quite a while, and they were never caught. Tom and I didn't find out about this illegal activity until long after.

Positive thinking and huge denial mechanisms also helped Christopher. He was sure he would beat the cancer just as he had survived his heart failure. He was always saying, "When I beat this cancer,

I am going to..." He was always sure there was going to be life after this cancer.

Our family coped by creating homes in the strangest places. Our family home became wherever Christopher was—a University of Washington Medical Center ICU room for six weeks in 1997 or a cancer facility apartment in Seattle for three months in 2004. There were also several shorter stays at St. Peter Hospital, UW Hospital, and the final week when we took over the patient waiting room on the oncology floor back in Olympia at St. Peter. Jeff enjoyed making these settings less institutional for his brother by bringing in large video game consoles and all the necessary wires. (Remember, this was 2004.) Jeff even took closet door handles off so posters hung correctly. He and Christopher had little regard for the routines and rules of hospitals, and they actually took great pride in this.

Christopher in his bed was the center, and we, the family, slept in chair beds, on squeaky, lumpy cots, on waiting rooms couches, and even in straight-backed chairs—wherever we had to be. Our physical environment was so much less important than the fact we were together.

Chapter 16

Déjà Vu All Over Again

One day Christopher decided he was going to write a book. He asked that we purchase a handheld digital recorder in March 2004 so he could record what was happening as well as his thoughts and feelings going through the stem cell transplant. He started out with excitement in his voice.

The gloomy weather is in line with how I feel. It's kinda shitty outside, and…um…it's kind of shitty inside me.

Walking along the concourse at the UW Medical Center, everything screams nostalgia. I mean everything—from the way the skylights shine light onto the motley [chuckling] characters that walk along with a constant ebb and flow to the [chuckling] exhausted doctors and family members taking breaks on the spacious couches. There is a huge part of me that is deeply, deeply grateful to this place because this May 31 will be the seventh anniversary of the heart transplant I received here. For the last seven years, every time I've walked on this concourse it's either been to get checkups and told I'm healthy or to come in to be repaired.

It's [sigh] such a conflicted, conflicted flood of emotions right now because I'm coming here to get an echocardiogram, which hopefully figures out what's causing these irregularities in my heart rate. At the same time, I know full well that walking down this particular concourse isn't going to be a quick fix this time. There's no way my cardiologist can, you know, draw some blood and tell me I'm all better.

I'm not going to leave the cardiology clinic today with a clean bill of health and feeling like a million bucks. There's also a large part of me that gets a huge, warm fuzzy feeling from being here and knowing full well these people are the best at what they do.

I've got to go to the fourth floor here in the next few minutes to get an echocardiogram. And, of course, echocardiograms are one of my favorite things in the entire world (not) because it was what initially diagnosed my heart failure. Two weeks later it landed me in the ICU up here at UW. Ever since then I've kind of been understandably soured on the procedure. With it being the harbinger of doom for my heart, it's bittersweet to be here, and I don't imagine it'll get any sweeter or better.

Have you ever had déjà vu so strong it feels as if it could crawl down your throat and choke you? Or, by the same token, had déjà vu so strong that the sounds and sights and smells hurl you into the past? And the fact is that I really want to be in that past rather than this present.

The very smell and the sounds of the cardiology clinic on four north—the waiting room, the smell of the isolation mask on my face— it all feels so familiar and so reassuring. Four north was a place that was initially really very painful and sad for me, and then it became a place that [sigh] *always was a good thing for five-plus years.*

It seems as if the only thing that has changed is my circumstance, and so the intensity of these conflicting emotions is about enough to tear me in two. I want to smile about remembering, and I also want to cry about having to be here again with yet another life-threatening condition. It's very odd [sigh]*, but the déjà vu is ultimately more positive than negative. Right now I'm so browbeaten, and my emotional buffers are so low.* [Sigh.] *It is a mind-fuck-and-a-half, and we expect it's far from over.*

Christopher had the echocardiogram and came out extremely agitated.

Wasn't that just fucking special? Oh fuck! [Stifled sob.] *You know, when they call things such as echocardiograms noninvasive medicine, it's good to take that term with a grain of salt. For me anyway an echocardiogram hurts like a fucking bastard. It's one of the most unmitigated forms of torture I have to endure. I mean, you're lying flat for over an hour in various positions while this strobe that sees through your chest is raked across your side. Basically if they cannot see through, they have to push harder, and they have to squish it around in order to make the view clear up. I'm not real skinny, so I've got plenty of meat, and my heart is in a funny spot because it's not mine. It's just...it's fucking agony.*

[Sighing and calming down a bit.] *Thankfully I had some music to listen to. I had also taken two Percocet, so I was relatively comfortable. It's just...if there is a hell for me, it's getting a fucking echocardiogram.*

I was telling my mom a few minutes ago that I've got a lot of animosity and hatred built up for this place because of everything I had to go through prior to and during my transplant. There was a long time when I couldn't even stand looking at this building much less coming within miles of it. The first few years, the only times I came here were when I was sick or broken, and they fixed me up. For the last three or so years, every time I came up here (and I mean every time), I've been told I'm the picture of health—the epitome of everything a healthy transplant patient should and needs to be. [Sigh.]

Now I've got this new life-threatening illness, and it has brought up all these emotions and past experiences from the previous illness. Now I've got this new illness and the fact I'm going to have to stay here through my stem cell transplant. It's also right fucking in the middle of spring—just like last time! With all those things combined and the fact that everything's the same—everything smells the same and looks the same and sounds the same—I get this odd sensation that I'm walking through my past. The membrane between the present and the past is so thin I could almost poke through it and, you know, coexist at the same time.

I'm in this maelstrom of thoughts, emotions, remembrances, and déjà vu, and there's no way for me to split them up and cordon them off into their own unique spaces. They are all mixed together in one, and there's no way I can differentiate, so there are times when it's like I'm getting ambushed by myself. [Stifled sob.] *I get ambushed by it all, and I find myself at the same time fondly reminiscing about a place that I'm very distrustful and hateful of—all within the context of being scared fucking shitless about what's happening to me right this second!*

I'm already having to deal with the baggage I have about spring from the last, you know, seven years. I wish there was a way I could effectively separate and tease out and find where each of these individual emotions is coming from. They are all so effectively mixed in together that it...I...I'm just overwhelmed. As a result it's going to be very, very hard to maintain my focus on what is happening in the present.

My immediate trouble is my stem cell transplant and beating this cancer, but the emotional context is already so incredibly crowded.

So now I'm sitting out in front of the SCCA in the nice cool air, and I feel as if I can breathe again. It's been a trying day. There's a sense that if I could just have a huge cry, it would make things a lot better, but logically I know that's not the case. I mean, it's not going to change any circumstance or anything. There's...[Sigh.] I don't know. If my sighs and pauses could only say what they mean, you know? There's so much of this process that's beyond. Beyond words. Beyond my ability to express.

This whole recording process makes things [chuckling] harder than they have to be, but that doesn't necessarily mean it's not super valuable and can someday be put toward this book. Hopefully all these recordings will come together to be some good to somebody someday. Although ultimately it might be cathartic for me, it's really hard right now to regurgitate all these emotions so, so quickly after feeling them, but...uh...I imagine I will get better at it as the days progress.

Chapter 17

It's Not "We"; It's "Me"

The following are more recordings from Christopher as the stem cell process began:

March 23—Day One

Day one was my initial consult up at the Seattle Cancer Care Alliance (SCCA) for the stem cell transplant. We met with the physician's assistant and did a meet and greet with everybody except for my primary physician. I felt awful after we were done. At about 5:00 p.m., I started getting an elevated heart rate and feeling really, really bad. Everything was presenting itself like a heart failure issue. I was short of breath with movement, and my heart rate was 120.

The next morning when I woke up my heart rate was still the same. We called, and they had us come into triage early in the morning. I was there for the next nine hours. I was extremely dehydrated, and my lab work was all fucked up from last week's chemo. They started a liter of fluid and gave me two units of packed cells. They're going to send me home with a mini-pump to finish the liter of fluid. I feel a million billion percent better.

March 24—Day Two

Hello. This is day two and night two, and I am starting the recording for the new book Painkillers and Gummi Bears. I have had far too much

Ativan to attempt this technical procedure at the moment. It is important, however, to start nonetheless, and start I have. More tomorrow. Bye.

March 26—Day Four

This morning I had a little laugh attack when we got in the shuttle van to the SCCA. [Chuckling.] *Eddie, the shuttle bus driver, is an incredibly nice guy, and he has decided that KBSG, the Oldies, is the best, most uplifting music station for the shuttle. We had "Crocodile Rock" by Elton John come on the radio, and you know what that song is like. It's like a carnival! It's like da da da da da, and it just struck me as so funny because we were a van full of cancer patients going to the cancer hospital. Nothing about it even remotely seemed like a "Crocodile Rock" morning. Silly, silly stuff. My mom tried to hush up my little hysterical laugh, but when has that ever worked?* [Laughing.]

March 27—Day Five

Everything's good today. I feel good today. It's weird. You think you feel fine, and then you get a couple units of blood, and you feel really good. It changes your perspective a little bit on everything. It's an incredibly helpful mechanism of the body that you never actually know how bad you feel until you feel better again. If you did know, you'd spend a lot of time dwelling on the crappy times.

March 28—Day Six

Lacey called me. This is the girl my age. We met the first day while I was up here in the waiting room. She had her stem cell transplant a year ago. She had a twelve percent chance of a cure, and she is doing great. She came and picked me up, and we went back to her apartment. We basically just traded stories for about, I don't know, three hours. It's uncanny how similar our experiences are. Her birthday is October thirteenth; mine's the twentieth. She had her first stem cell transplant on April 1, and my crash day was April seventh. I mean, it was just uncanny when she was talking about how springtime was a tough time for her because this was the period of time she went through her big medical travails. I was just kind of taken aback at that because I don't think I've ever met anybody I could even compare my story to, much less have so many parallels. I managed to get out of there at, I don't know, sometime after midnight.. It was good to stay up late and be out of the place with someone my own age.

March 29—Day Seven

[Quieter and in a wistful tone.] *I felt good today. You know, I only need one or two of those a month. That's all it takes to remind you. [Choking up a bit.] Remind you why you're fighting tooth and nail to stay alive. It's not a…it's not a battle worth fighting unless you can get at least a glimpse of what you're fighting for.*

There are a lot of people here I think who don't get one day a month or one day every two months. The health they are fighting to regain is so far off it's a foreign concept. Some of these people make me look like a total wuss as far as endurance or resolve goes. I doubt I would be able to do it like those people—to maintain my resolve. I certainly don't want to have to see if I can. I don't want to have to go there.

March 30—Day Eight

I'm keeping it together really well. I'm very proud of myself. I had a little bit of a cranky time yesterday. I think I might be getting a little addicted to the Percocet and/or Vicodin—the narcotic painkillers I've been taking, but that is no surprise to me. It's a reality of this situation. I don't really care. I will gladly be a drug addict until the day this cancer's over. The benefits of taking those painkillers that make me feel better greatly outweigh any detriment I am going to face after this cancer. I might have to go into a rubber room for a while, but that's whatever.

Um…my mom has a diametrically different view of the whole thing, but I don't really care. Comfort comes so few and far between these days. What little comfort I can draw from anything, I'm more than willing to do, and damn the consequences until a later time. I honestly can't imagine beating cancer and then after beating cancer having a tough time getting off painkillers. It's apples and oranges. On a scale of one to ten, it's about a nine to beat the cancer and about a one to get off painkillers, so that's all right.

March 31—Day Nine

There's no psychological difficulties with being here at the SCCA today. It's just long because it takes two or two and a half hours to infuse a unit of blood, and that's, you know, per unit. I'm getting two units of blood and a bag of 'lytes. That's five hours. Five hours is a long time. I mean, that's why we moved up to Seattle. To be close to here so I could have all these procedures and stuff like this done, but still it's hard to…uh…it's hard to see spending five hours in a bed being infused with bags of fluids as a normal day. [Chuckling.] "Normal" is a wonderful word, but…uh…what some people call "normal" is so crazy, and what other people call normal is actually normal. You know? Mom cooking dinner every night is my normal.

April 1—Day Ten

I keep saying "we." I need to stop saying that. I need to specify. I alternate between feeling as if I'm going through this with a team to feeling like, no. This is all really just happening to me. If everything fails, I'm going to be the one who dies.

So it would be really helpful if I could stop using "we" for everything because it's "me." That's the harsh reality of it.

I don't know if it's mental. My mind is skipping a step just trying to keep me comfortable, so I don't dwell on the fact that this treatment is the final battle ground. Ultimately if I stop thinking of everything in terms of the team or the family, then if not easier, it'll be better. It will help me focus my thoughts and feelings about this situation and hopefully help me transfer them clearly to this format—this little recorder.

As the weeks progressed and Christopher got sicker, his levity vanished. I took over the little recorder and started documenting some of the process.

"Christopher was in the hospital for chemo, and he woke up about 5:30 a.m. after a combination of a horrible dream and hallucination. It terrified him, and he was trembling. He said he was looking at his heart monitor while lying in the ICU, and the monitor started flat-lining, and he knew he was dying.

"The nurse went to get him some Ativan to help settle down. While he was waiting for the medication, he asked me for his iPod, and he turned on our favorite boat vacation Chuck Mangione song. It's the song we play every year as we make it to our destination on the boat. The nurse came back with the medication, and listening to that soothing song, Christopher slowly settled back down and fell into a deep sleep. This morning the nurses were kind enough to let him sleep almost all morning.

"Watching my son's hands shake as he took his iPod and turned on that music and knowing the stark terror he felt for his own impending death was my hardest moment so far. I wanted so much to take that terror away—to take on this cross for him. I would have done anything to change what was happening. I knew most clearly at that moment that no matter how much *we* all did what we could, Christopher was really facing this alone."

Chapter 18

Kicked in the Teeth—Hard
and Several Times

April 2—Day Eleven

I was told today my white blood cell count is high enough to start harvesting stem cells for the transplant. This is done through a process called apheresis. Blood is continually drawn out through my Hickman IV catheter in my chest, spun through a machine where the stem cells are captured, and then the blood is returned. I am very excited for this process to begin, as it is one step closer to beating this cancer. We start tomorrow morning!

April 3—Day Twelve

It was day two of apheresis, and I thought they had me down on the schedule for 9:00 a.m., Saturday, but we weren't sure. Everybody we called said eight o'clock. We got in there at about 8:00 a.m. and found out we weren't supposed to be there until nine. Damn. I could have slept another hour!

Once we started apheresis, it became apparent this was going to be an extremely long process, and we found out shortly that my Hickman IV catheter is very positional, so I couldn't sit up. I had to lie extremely reclined if not completely flat in order for the blood to appropriately go in and out of the apheresis machine. So I was very unhappy with that. I also had some pretty intense stomach pain going on because I felt as if I had a huge turd stuck sideways.

We didn't finish apheresis until about 5:00 p.m., and I still needed the unit of blood. I couldn't get it at the SCCA, so I had to go to the UW Hospital for the second time in two days. Damn.

I came back to the apartment in between for about forty-five minutes. I took a couple milligrams of Ativan and a couple Marinols, and I ate a big-ass weed cookie just to calm down. At about 5:45, we headed over to the UW to get the blood infused. Unfortunately the UW has a different protocol for infusing blood products that is really slow. Instead of a two-hour infusion for a unit of blood, it ballooned into a three-hour infusion. I have tried to be a good sport all day, but when you've already spent eight hours screwing around trying to get your apheresis done, an extra hour for a blood transfusion is not a real copasetic option. It was about 9:30 p.m. before the blood was done infusing, and we managed to get the hell out of there.

Of course, it was daylight saving, so on top of a shitty fourteen-hour day of medical hell, I lost an hour of sleep. Thank God I was settled down by the time I went to bed.

Sunday morning I had a much better idea of what the day was going to entail. You know, when you feel as if everything is completely out of your control, the smallest modicum of...not control...but knowing what's going to happen makes you feel as if you're exercising at least a little bit of control over the situation, so I was feeling much better about it.

April 6—Day Fifteen

We had the pre-transplant [pre–stem cell transplant] *informed consent conference. We met with Dr. Holmberg and Rick (the primary nurse). Dr. Holmberg did the full informed consent for the stem cell transplant and followed what was on the written informed consent Dad, Mom, and I had seen about a month ago. Jeff, unfortunately, had not seen that document, and he didn't really know the full extent* of everything that could happen because of the stem cell. Jeffrey got very pale and light-headed and thought he was going to pass out.

He managed to stay upright. The doctor asked him if he was OK once, and he said he was. It wasn't until after the conference that we realized Jeff really didn't understand the full extent of the severity of this and all the complications that could happen.

I am really worried about Jeff. He's really, really, really worked up. My personal opinion is that he had a barrier between my illness and his normal everyday work life because there was the sixty-mile distance between Seattle and Olympia. Now we're up here, it's different. He has no ability to separate dealing with my illness and work, so I think that's the root of a lot of his stress. I told him I thought he'd sleep a lot better if he came over here. I think he feels more comfortable when he's in close proximity to me. Among other things, I've also got more than enough Ativan to go around, so we…uh…could drug him up to his max. [Chuckling.]

April 7—Day Sixteen

I continue to have really awful side pain associated with my tumors. At this point I'm completely convinced my tumors are growing, and so I'm just beside myself trying to go to bed. I'm getting all teary and extremely, extremely worried. Mom and Dad are in bed already, and I am sitting here by myself. You know, it's hard not to just feel a bit sorry for yourself in this situation.

April 10—Day Nineteen

All right. It is now Saturday afternoon. Fuck. That would make it day nineteen. OK. So I haven't recorded in a few days. I've got a lot of good things to talk about and a lot of bad things.

Monday night we received a call I had indeed collected all my stem cells—a full 5.2 million to be exact. This is a bonus and a fuckin' half without any doubt. So that night Mom got up, and we all went out to Azteca and had some Mexican food. I ended up not eating that much, and I felt kind of crappy afterward, but, you know,

I was still having lots of bone pain from the G-shots, and I just felt pretty puny from all the apheresis. I still have that side pain. It's getting worse and scaring the hell out of me.

Tuesday morning we got up and went to get my blood drawn at about noon and then came back. I hopped on and played several hours of Counter-Strike *and kept it low-key. Wednesday we did a repeat of the same. Jesse and Terry were planning on coming up Wednesday night, staying through Thursday, and leaving Thursday evening.*

Jesse and Terry showed up right before South Park, *so we ended up watching it and then the* Dave Chappelle Show, *which was just downright hysterical. We had a good time. I mean, just sitting around bullshitting with my friends is invaluable to me. It's a great help for my attitude.*

So we wanted to make plans for Thursday, but I got a call from SCCA that pissed me off. They were supposed to not do anything on Thursday and restart everything on Friday. So they called me on Thursday saying I needed to get some labs done, and then I needed a CT at 11:30. [Sigh.] *So we ended up going in on Thursday.*

After the CT scan, we headed right back up to triage. They ended up writing me prescription for a couple milligrams of morphine to take the edge off the side pain. It did a pretty good job. Then we were waiting for the results of the CT.

About twenty or twenty-five minutes later, Dr. Holmberg came in with a very serious look on her face. She closed the drapes, sat down, and turned off the TV. "Well, I've got some bad news," she said.

It was just me and my mom at this point, and we were a bit taken aback by this. The doctor proceeded to tell us that my tumors had continued to grow throughout the ICE chemo—the first chemo in the stem cell transplant process. My main mass was 20 percent larger than it was a month ago, and I had new tumors presenting themselves along the bottom side of my diaphragm.

What this translated to was that she wanted to get me in the hospital and on the type of chemotherapy regimen I had been on in January through the end of March. Then once that was done, instead of giving the normal month for the body to recuperate, we were going in and doing the stem cell transplant.

The doctor said this changed some things. By adding extra chemo and moving up the transplant, we were increasing the mortality rate for the stem cell transplant from 10 percent to 15 percent, and what we were looking at now was that the stem cell transplant had only a 20 percent chance of working.

Now this was not good news. So Mom and I were kind of, I mean…like a ton of bricks. Yeah. It's like getting kicked in the teeth but really hard and several times. So we were pretty much losing our cool at this point. As crazy and serendipitous as it might sound, Pastor Nelson showed up just as Dr. Holmberg came in, so he overheard most of the conversation, and he was there as soon as she left. He was there for my initial reaction—complete and utter despair.

It was one of those moments where all perspective went out the window. There was no perspective whatsoever. There are all these extremely good, rational things I tell myself again and again that I really do believe in and that help me keep going. There's things such as, "You're stronger than this." I mean, that all sounded so trite and so hollow at this point. We all had a good cry, and I ended up taking some drugs. For that period of time, Mom and I pretty much had me all but buried, and it was, you know, just a reaction we had to have.

It wasn't good, and we said a little prayer, and before we said a little prayer, Dianna [the triage nurse] *came in and heard the story and gave me a pep talk. She said how she was going to pray for me and how today was a good day for grieving and crying. But tomorrow we would wake up with good outlooks, and it would be a serene day—a day to get on with things and get ready to beat this bitch!*

In our prayer we asked for serenity and grace and for God to look over us. That was probably the first time I had really prayed in many, many years. I kind of wondered if prayer under duress holds any less weight, but I don't know. I'm not going to propose I have an answer to that.

Then I talked to Jeff, and he was all, "What can I do for you?" and I was like, "Well, you can take the rest of the day off work and come be with me."

Dr. Holmberg said we could decide what to do. I had the option of waiting until Saturday to get the chemotherapy, or I could have a night to chill back at the apartment, relax, and mull things over and then go in Friday morning to get the chemotherapy started. Of course, I had the option of not doing anything at all and resigning myself to death. That is a fucking stupid option. No, no, no.

We are going to get right up in this cancer's face and not give it any more time than we have to. I know they've got to give you options, but I'm twenty-two, and I've got so much more fight in me, it isn't even funny. So I told the doctor that I wanted to spend the night at the apartment and then go in for chemo on Friday.

Back at the apartment, I called Dad up, and he gave me a great pep talk. He said we had all gone through this grieving, crying, and putting you in the ground thing so many times that he was just not going there anymore. We were walking out of the clinic and it was going to work, and that was the end of it, and there were no two or three or four or six ways about it. That was just the way it was going to be.

That was exactly what I needed to hear. My dad has been my rock of support throughout this, and as far as pep talks go, it was about as good as they come. About the time we get off the phone with Dad, Jeff showed up, and we had a big hug, and Jeff and Mom ate some salad, chips, salsa, and whatnot. All the while I'm kind of waiting for the oral Dilaudid they gave me to take effect.

I finally calmed down, and I was exhausted. Completely and utterly exhausted. This was the end of a really fucked-up day. We turned off the lights after Conan O'Brien's show and went to sleep.

By Friday we were in much better spirits and putting all this into more perspective and more of a positive spin. Dr. Harlan called and told me that a 20 percent chance of a cure didn't sound like much unless you were one of the 20 percent. Then it was 100 percent. That buoyed our spirits and recommitted us. Our resolve was back, and we were Ready to go forward.

Chapter 19

Cancer Equals Sick

I used the recorder when Christopher was too sick to bother with it.

May 26—Day Nine (post-stem cell transplant)

"It has been over a month since we have recorded. Christopher had what we called 'killer chemo" which wipes out the bone marrow and all blood forming cells and, hopefully, all the cancer. A few days after this they transfused the stem cells they collected back into his body. We are now in the stage where we wait for Christopher's bone marrow to start producing blood cells again.

He has been very sick for the past three weeks. He's got stage four mucositis. This means he has a very raw throat and mouth, and he has to use a large suction catheter to clear his secretions. It's not uncommon for him to suction up quite a bit of blood and tissue trying to expectorate this very, very thick, really tenacious mucus. He's taking a high dose of IV Dilaudid for the pain, and he's fairly well controlled on that except when he coughs. There's nothing that takes away that pain.

"He has not been able to swallow anything for four or five days. He's really thirsty and insists on having a fresh Pepsi (his favorite beverage) on ice sitting by his bedside at all times, even though he can't drink it. This simple symbol of his normal life, within reach but impossible for him to enjoy, rips my heart out. To me it epitomizes everything lost. It is the essence of *Painkillers and Gummi Bears*—his total loss of innocence, youth, and health. A mother cannot deal with this.

"He also has had a really rapid heart rate for the last three or four days. It's about 140 beats a minute when he's just lying quietly, and it goes up to about 160 when he gets up to go to the bathroom.

"His liver and kidneys are not working well due to the hit from the 'killer chemo.' The metabolites from the chemo tend to destroy or damage the small vessels in the liver, and that causes an outlet obstruction, and fluid can't flow through the liver as it should. The kidneys start hoarding water and sodium, and Christopher's body is hoarding about twenty pounds of fluid right now. He is getting a ton of IV medications and nutrition that worsen the fluid retention problem.

"He is running a fever ranging from 102 to 104 degrees. One minute he is shivering and freezing cold and requires six blankets, and then he is dying of the heat and stripping everything off with ice packs stuck in his armpits and groin.

"He must get up and shower once a day. This makes him so cold and miserable—even when we wrap him up in heated blankets before and after. His feet and hands are swollen, red, and blistered, so getting out of bed is excruciating.

"In addition to his mouth, throat, hands, and feet, he has extremely swollen and inflamed testicles. Christopher had to have two weeks of radiation on his testicles before the stem cell transplant because cancer cells can hide there. This procedure was quite humiliating for Christopher, and his gallows humor kicked in. 'Testicles' became 'toas-ticles,' 'the toasties,' or 'my toasted nuts.'

"The radiation oncologist said there would be no side effects to this treatment. 'He'll hardly even notice it,' the doctor said. I don't know if he was clueless or lying, but Christopher's testicles are bright red and the size of grapefruits. The physician's assistant examined Christopher and said it was common for them to get sore and swollen. The RadiaGel they gave us for 'irritation' has been applied every day and hasn't seemed to do anything.

"The last few days, one of the things that has been so miserable is that he oozes blood from his nose. Then it gets all plugged up, he can't breathe, and he feels really claustrophobic. The only thing that cures it is when he gets enough platelets. Then his nose seems to clear up, and he can breathe through it. They think his body is destroying so many platelets because his temperature is so high.

"So, for the past six weeks, Christopher has been very ill, and since May 9, he has been deathly ill. He has been a man of few words, but through it all he's been a real champ. He is, however, just sick of it. He's really, really, sick of it.

"We are all praying the stem cells will start working. Once they do his body will begin to heal itself. We pray this procedure that has almost killed him will also kill the cancer."

Chapter 20

Just Tell Me Stories

The morning of June 4 started as many others in the post-stem cell phase, and I made this short recording:

"This is the morning of June 4, and Christopher ate an entire bowl of Cream of Wheat for breakfast. When I asked him how it tasted, he said it 'tasted like ass,' but I don't care what it tasted like as long as he ate it."

Christopher hadn't eaten anything in days. I was ecstatic he'd had some cereal. I knew he was still very sick, but I prayed we were close to a turnaround. The next day I found out how desperately wrong I was.

The physicians came in that Friday morning and told us we needed to have a family conference at 3:00 p.m. to talk about "care planning." *Care planning,* I wondered. What in the world was a care planning conference going to be about right now? Something felt really off, and I called Tom and Jeff. I told them to get to the hospital right away. Christopher's fluid status was horrible. He could hardly breathe because of so much fluid in his lungs, and he now had thirty-five pounds of excess fluid in his body. However, his lab work wasn't bad at all, and his hands and feet had finally started to heal. Underneath the blistered skin was new soft skin—a sign of healing. We were still hopeful.

When Tom got to the hospital, Christopher said he wanted to go for a walk. He was probably thinking if he could still walk, the news from the doctors couldn't be too bad. He managed, through superhuman effort, to walk two loops around the nursing unit. This was unbelievable. He had barely been able to get into and out of the shower the previous few days. Jeff arrived, and we nervously waited until 3:00 p.m.

The attending physician was Finnish and a very kind, compassionate person. He sat down and told Christopher it was time to stop. Treatment had failed, and he needed to get home to say good-bye to his family and friends because he had only a few days to live. The CT scans they had taken to look for an infection showed tumors that continued to grow and were now in his liver and throughout his abdomen.

I have no recollection of what happened for the next few hours. I think my body protected me from these most painful moments. Jeff helped me remember his own reaction.

"I remember my chin fell to my chest," Jeff said, "and I felt as if I was a blow-up doll that was starting to deflate. There was always a plan. There was always one more thing to try. A trick up someone's sleeve. We had lived for so long with Christopher on the edge of death that I couldn't believe the end had come. No more options. Five to seven days, the doctor said. We got a five- to seven-day heads-up. It was as if we missed one mortgage payment and were being foreclosed. As if we had been living on credit cards and had reached the max.

I don't remember Christopher's initial reaction to the news or anyone else's. I could only take this news into my own brain without any capacity to care how anyone else took it. It was as if we were all in the room alone getting this information. It felt like being in the center of an explosion when there is no sound and everything is white, and then slowly the sound and the color returns. The end. The fucking end of my brother's life."

A medical miracle had not prevailed. All the misery and suffering Christopher had gone through with the stem cell transplant was for naught. After seven years and well over a million dollars of health care, Christopher was going to die.

The doctors stressed that there wasn't much time left, and if Christopher wanted to see his friends, family, and home, we needed to act now. The social worker said that with the weekend coming, it would be Monday before we could mobilize the resources for care in Olympia.

I told them I wanted Christopher to go home on hospice if at all possible. His care would be a huge challenge as he was so big and nearly immobile. I talked to the executive director of Providence Hospice, and she was optimistic we could work this out.

After the care team left, Christopher looked dazed as if sucker punched. He asked Jeff to dig out his list of friends' phone numbers and call them with the bad news. He was very worried about how they would take it. Jeff asked if I could go with him. As Jeff was walking out the door, I sat down on Christopher's bed. "Honey," I said, "how are you doing with this news?" My heart was breaking. I couldn't ask the straight question—how do you feel about dying?

He just shook his head as if trying to clear his thoughts. "I can't quite get my head around it." He paused a moment. "It isn't like I never thought about this possibility, Mom."

I kissed and hugged him and told him I wouldn't leave his side. I told him I loved him so very much.

Tom stayed with Christopher while Jeff and I went outside by a gazebo. It was a beautiful day. Jeff sat on the grass and started calling, and I lay on a nearby bench. Jeff called Chris's close friends, and each time he shared the news, it was like a reality punch in his gut.

"Terry, this is Jeff."

"Hey, Jeff," Terry said. He was glad to hear from him. "What's up?"

"Treatment has failed, and Christopher's not going to make it. We are bringing him home."

"Five to eight times I had to give that message," Jeff later said. "Five to eight times. It was brutal."

A few hours later, I fell asleep on the bed chair, and when I awoke Jeff and Christopher were watching *Lord of the Rings*. I heard the following conversation:

"So, Boy [Jeff's favorite nickname for Christopher], what do you want to have happen? Do you want to be buried or cremated?" Jeff asked his brother in a matter-of-fact voice.

"I guess cremated," Christopher said.

"Where do you want your ashes spread?" Jeff continued.

"Some at Shallow Bay on Sucia Island and at the lighthouse on Stuart Island, I think. Oh yeah, some at Saddlebag Island also. And take some with you when you sail around the world."

"So, what do you want to do with your life insurance?" Jeff asked.

"I want you to have it," Christopher said. "Use it for your trip or whatever."

There were many awkward pauses throughout the conversation.

"I want to write my own eulogy," Christopher told his brother. "I think that is important. I don't want to do it right now, but I do want to do it."

Jeff later asked Christopher if he was ready, but he never wrote anything.

I was pretending I was asleep because I didn't want to stop this honest conversation, but Jeff could see the tears streaming down my face.

Christopher was hardly awake all weekend. I feared he would not regain consciousness again. I was telling my concerns to the Physician's Assistant (PA), and she said she had frequently seen this happen. Once the fight was over, the patient oftentimes lapses into a totally introverted space. I remember sobbing and feeling I hadn't said what I wanted to say if I never got another chance to talk with my son.

All weekend the staff shared their condolences with us, and they told us how much they had enjoyed taking care of Christopher. Monday was a day for transfer plans. After a realistic assessment of Christopher's care needs, we decided he should go to Providence St. Peter Hospital in Olympia. Tom, Jeff, and I were exhausted. All our fight had left us, and we didn't have the energy to become Christopher's primary caregivers at home.

We had to pack up the apartment at the Pete Gross House, and it was such a bittersweet experience. There were seventy-five get well cards taped to the walls along with prayer shawls, prayer blankets, spa packages, CDs, a freezer full of casseroles, Costco snacks, and a drawer full of Dove chocolate—all given in love to us by friends and family. We were listless and frozen with grief, and packing felt overwhelming. I didn't want to leave because this had been our cocoon—the place where

Christopher was going to beat this cancer. To leave only reinforced that the end was near. How was a mother supposed to handle this? I thought this through my exhausted fog. I could hardly put one foot in front of the other or have a coherent thought. I didn't feel as if I was in any shape for the final days. Family pitched in to help us on the Seattle end, while our church friends pitched in on the Olympia end.

In anticipation of us coming home, our friends flew into a frenzy at our home. They tore out the carpet in our family room and put in Pergo flooring. They built a ramp to get Christopher into the family room, mowed the lawn, bought flower baskets, and stocked the house with food. Jeff was there recording with the camcorder, and as he taped he called this "getting ready for the return of the king." It was such a gift of love. What a loving community we were part of. Jeff has since remarked that there were probably thousands of little and big kindnesses we weren't even aware of. He still feels it is important we realize that and continue to pay it forward to others.

Tuesday morning on June 7 my sister arrived early before we left for Olympia. She brought a small container of fresh fruit in hopes Christopher might have a bit of an appetite. Christopher emerged from his three-day coma looking fresh, calm, and ready for the day. He welcomed his Auntie Chris with a big joyful hug and kiss and thanked her for the fruit. He ate a strawberry and savored it. "This tastes fantastic," he said. I was shocked.

I wish I had the right words to describe how Christopher was that entire day. His eyes were bright, he smiled and laughed a lot, and he was alert and helpful. He was totally in the present moment. It was as if the weight of the last seven years of fighting for life had been lifted, and he was free. It was such a gift. My heart was soaring. I had been preparing for Christopher to be afraid to die, but this was totally the opposite. He had had enough and was ready to go home, see his friends, and end the fight. We cleaned him up and got him ready for the move to Olympia.

My sister's husband, Uncle Tom, was a firefighter and paramedic, and he had arranged a medic van to transport Christopher to St. Peter Hospital in Olympia. Uncle Tom and his coworker showed up about midmorning. Christopher stood (shocking considering how sick he was) and got on the gurney. He was very happy to see his favorite uncle and thanked him for caring for him while the coworker drove. "It is an honor, Chris," Tom said.

I got to ride home in the medic van right next to Christopher. Uncle Tom had some narcotics he used a few times to keep Christopher comfortable. It was a stunningly beautiful sunny warm day—so unusual in the Pacific Northwest in June. The sun seemed a fitting background to the joyful occasion of going home. I listened and watched in awe as Christopher and his uncle talked openly and honestly about the end of treatment and impending death.

Uncle Tom told stories of when Christopher was a little guy. Christopher looked radiant, and he laughed and fully enjoyed this. They shared their love for each other openly and unabashedly, and our tears flowed freely. They were tears of sadness but also of love and joy. In those moments everything was just as it was supposed to be, and there was perfect peace and love. Again I knew there was so much more going on than simply the physical plane. I knew God had us in the palm of his hand.

Jeff remembers a phone call with Christopher as Jeff was driving his truck full of Peter Gross House belongings directly behind the medic van. I must have dialed and handed Christopher the phone, but I don't remember.

"Hey. What's up?" said Christopher is his full, booming, healthy voice. "I see you behind us. Isn't it just a beautiful day?"

Jeff nearly dropped the phone. The day before Christopher had been semicomatose and unable to communicate. Jeff told me later, "It was like he was back and happy and fully himself. It was such a gift."

We got to St. Peter Hospital, and Uncle Tom kissed Christopher on the forehead as he left him in his room on the oncology floor. Jeff showed up shortly after and plastered an enormous banner over the entire wall facing Christopher's bed. Jeff had taken a photo to Kinkos. It was of Shallow Bay, Sucia Island, in the San Juan Islands. Year after year many idyllic vacation days had been spent there fishing, crabbing, beachcombing, and swimming. The picture was of one of the many sunsets viewed from our boat.

Jeff said he walked into Kinkos, went up to a woman at the counter, and said, "Here is the deal. My little brother is dying of cancer in the hospital, and has less than two weeks to live. This is a picture of where we went as kids, and I want to blow it up as big as possible so it can go on the wall in his hospital room. I don't care what it costs, but I want my brother to look at this instead of a sterile hospital room wall."

The woman was very touched and worked for hours using special filters and a matte finish. She constructed a seven-feet long and five-feet tall masterpiece from the small four by six photo taken from our home photo album.

Christopher was asleep when Jeff brought it in. Jeff worked quickly with Velcro to paste it on the wall that Christopher looked at from his bed. When he woke up and saw it, he couldn't have been more delighted. "That is so fucking cool!" He studied it for a moment with a huge smile on his face. "That is totally awesome!" he told his brother.

Jeff stood there beaming with tears running down his cheeks. "Christopher," said Jeff, "what else can we do for you?"

"Just get my friends in here and tell me stories," Christopher replied.

"You got it," Jeff said. "Everyone already knows you are in Olympia, and they should start coming soon."

"Perfect," Christopher said as he nodded off for a nap.

He had been admitted and had a pain pump set up. He was comfortable. By this time he could not go very long at all without a substantial amount of pain medication, and we were liberal with it. Anxiety and pain were not an option, and the medication took care of both.

By that evening the CD player that had played soothing music in Seattle was rocking to hip-hop, and the room was full of Christopher's friends—up to fifteen at one time. This continued for the next three days. I was not privy to many of the stories that were told, but I caught a few. I was shocked to learn Christopher had lost his virginity when he was a freshman in high school to a freshman college woman. He had lied and told her he went to WSU and was home on break. Initially I was upset, and then I started laughing hysterically. There wasn't much I was going to do about it now! There were stories of crazy antics involving cars, boats, camping trips, and college parties. From out in the hall intermittent roars of laughter were audible after another good one had been told. It was obviously cathartic for everyone to have this time of togetherness and reminiscing. Tears flowed along with the laughter.

The musical thanatologist, Andrea, came every day to play the harp. She was part of the palliative care program, and her job was to play the harp for dying patients. She played for Christopher each day but not when he was listening to hip-hop with his "bros." Then she played for us in the waiting room, and it was soothing and wonderful. She commented more than once that we were giving Christopher a good death. "My job is to help people have peaceful deaths, and you all are doing it right," she said.

Pastor Nelson was a daily visitor, and on the first day in Olympia he brought communion to Christopher. Surprisingly Christopher had requested this. After his little wafer of bread and sip of wine, he promptly threw it up. He looked at David with concern and asked, "Does it still count?"

David chuckled. "Yes, Christopher. It is all good."

When Terry, one of Christopher's closest friends, came to visit Christopher, he was shocked by how changed and close to death he was. He hadn't seen him for several weeks and hardly recognized him. Tom was on duty at that point, and Terry, like most of Christopher's friends, had never been close to Tom. Terry was uncomfortable with the whole thing. Tom invited Terry over to the bed and got some lotion, and both took Christopher's hands and rubbed lotion into them. Terry told me recently that even though Christopher was not awake or speaking, he could see Christopher physically relax. It was a deep moment of communion with his friend and his friend's dad. Terry became a nurse many years later due to this experience.

The chemotherapy nurses who had treated Christopher in Olympia came with small presents for him, and the cafeteria workers from Yelm High School came to tell us how much they loved Christopher and how he had always made them feel special—especially when he mentioned them in his high school graduation speech. A good friend's mother brought a great big picture of Christopher and the "bros" in their high school graduation gowns with their arms around each other. Mementos, cards, and flowers kept piling up in the room.

Our church friends respected Christopher's privacy and would come see us in the family waiting room at the hospital. We took over that space for five days. All sorts of food was dropped off, and Jeff and his friends totally enjoyed this. There was even gin and tonic, and many freely imbibed. I can't believe the nursing staff let that happen. I know we weren't discreet, but nothing was said. Luckily from my days as a nursing supervisor, I knew everyone who worked in the hospital, and given our loss they bent over backward for us.

The puppies were brought up to say good-bye by the same friends who had brought them to Seattle for us. The puppies did not behave very well but got up on Christopher's bed so he could pet each of them good-bye.

All treatment was stopped when we got to St. Peter, so Christopher was getting no food or fluids. Because he had so much extra fluid when he arrived, this was not uncomfortable, and his breathing actually grew easier as time passed. The palliative care nurse helped regulate the pain medication for maximum comfort. She told me to tell Christopher that he could "go," as some patients hang on for their families.

One afternoon I was alone with Christopher, and it seemed like a good time to say this to Christopher. I whispered in his ear, "Christopher, I love you and want you to know that it is OK to go."

From what I thought was a coma, Christopher sat up a bit, opened his eyes as if he had just been taking a little nap, looked at me with anticipation, and said, "Go where?"

I did not know what to say to that, and I stuttered and stammered a bit. He soon closed his eyes again and was back asleep. I have laughed hysterically about this many times since.

The time I spent with him that week was often passed in peaceful silence. I felt a loving energy in the room that communicated all that was needed. We were at peace. Nothing more needed to be said. Christopher knew I loved him completely, and I knew he would always be with me—just not in this physical body.

As Pastor David went to Christopher's room one day, he stopped as he opened the door. Jeff was sitting next to Christopher's bed with his head on Christopher's arm. Jeff was weeping. David watched with tears in his eyes as Christopher slowly moved his other hand across his abdomen with great effort to cover Jeff's hand and gently pat him. My boys were never closer than at the end.

Chapter 21

June 13, 2004

Tom stayed at the hospital the night Christopher died. Before Jeff and I left on that last evening, Tom said, "I can't do this anymore."

Christopher had one more close friend to see, but he wasn't expected to arrive for two more days. Christopher had been on a constant pain medication infusion for days, and we had been increasing it slowly to make sure he was comfortable. By this time he could barely be aroused. He hadn't had anything to eat or drink for a week. The only time he stirred was when he had the urge to urinate, and we had to remind him to just let his urine go.

I told Tom to have the nurses increase the pain medication if he wanted. At this point we were all exhausted, and it was just a matter of hours or maybe a day. It might sound harsh, but it was time for it to be done. Tom told the nurses to increase the morphine drip, and they did.

Tom called at about 2:00 a.m. He said he had been sleeping but woke because he heard or felt a change in Christopher's breathing. It had changed markedly. As we talked on the phone, Christopher's breaths became short puffs of air until there were no more puffs. Tom said quietly that he was gone. I felt sick and scared and had to remind myself that it was indeed time to let him go. Now that the time had come, though, the finality of it took my breath away. Christopher was gone.

My primal response was *no*. I did not want my baby boy to die! How can a mother deal with this? Again I had to convince myself that the end of his suffering was what was most important. I took a moment for a quick prayer for help. I felt a sense of calm. That was God reminding me he was in charge, this was not the end, and I would get through this.

Jeff and I dressed hurriedly and drove to the hospital. We had to check in through the emergency room as it was the middle of the night. I will never forget the moment we entered the room. Jeff took one look at Christopher's lifeless body, and he made an animal like cry. He half-jumped and half-collapsed against the wall. Then he started sobbing loudly. It was so heartbreaking. He stayed there crumpled next to the beautiful wall-length picture he had made for his brother.

I stood there with tears streaming down my face. I held Christopher's hand. It felt so young with the new skin emerging after the horrible peeling from the stem cell transplant. My hand felt his face and head, and I could already detect a coolness. I had to actually watch him to be sure he wasn't breathing. Christopher had the blue blanket I had knit for him while sitting at his bedside draped over him. It was so important to me this blanket stay with him. I wanted my baby to be wrapped up in something I had made with all my love—even if it was an ineptly knit throw. One of us turned the CD player on to our favorite Chuck Mangione song. It was the one Christopher had turned to in his panic a few weeks before. This felt right.

Our pastor came, and we hugged and held each other. Pastor David knew the importance of presence and also knew there were no words to make anything better. David told us he was certain Christopher was at peace and that he indeed was now in the arms of God. We all cried, and then David said a short prayer over Christopher. Pastor David then put his hand on Christopher's forehead. As he made the sign of the cross, he said, "Christopher Thomas Stewart, child of God, you are sealed by the Holy Spirit and marked by the cross of Christ forever. Amen."

We bagged up all the belongings in the room and the many gifts and mementos brought by friends during Christopher's final week of life in Olympia. I had previously called the heart transplant service to see if they wanted to have Christopher's heart, and they confirmed it would be most helpful for research purposes. The head of pathology at St. Peter Hospital said he would personally take care of this for me. I was grateful.

It was time to head home. It was very hard to leave Christopher there. I didn't want to leave him, but I also knew he was no longer there in that cancer-ravaged human shell, and for that I was glad. He was done with the poisonous drugs and all the pain and suffering. He was free. I was happy for his freedom from suffering, but I knew a grief storm was brewing just over the horizon, and the worst time of my life was soon to begin.

When we got home from the hospital for the last time, it was about 4:00 a.m. The sun was coming up, and it was a beautiful morning. Jeff, Tom, and I cooked breakfast together and had screwdrivers before we went to sleep. Alcohol was an absolute necessity to all of us. We had to have something to numb our feelings. We actually joked, "Boy, this grief thing isn't so bad." We knew we were in a short, numbed lull before the storm. During breakfast we all sensed a great relief that Christopher's suffering was over. We then stumbled off to bed and slept for several hours.

We all felt we had said and done everything, and we knew Christopher had had the best death possible. Jeff later remarked, "If someone is dying of cancer, and you don't say what needs to be said, then it is on you, and you are an asshole."

There were no jagged edges in Christopher's death. It wasn't sudden or unexpected like a suicide or a car crash. We were able to give him a small country's worth of medical interventions, 100 percent support due to the flexibility of our jobs, great medical insurance, tons of family and friends, and enough Lutheran casseroles (as Jeff called them) to feed an army. A surplus of support blessed us, and we used every bit of it to make sure Christopher had a good death. This brought us much comfort over time, but in the moment it did little to ease the gut-wrenching pain.

Chapter 22

The Grief Delivery Truck Is Coming

The decision to turn up the narcotic medication haunted Tom for a very long time. I couldn't really understand why it bothered him so much, but now I think it had to do with Tom doing it because *he* couldn't stand it anymore. His weakness caused him to shorten his son's life by whatever brief amount of time might have been. In my mind we were shortening Christopher's suffering—not prematurely ending a life.

Monday we went to the mortuary, and afterward Tom and I went to Anthony's Home Port for lunch. We had screwdrivers, relaxed a bit, and actually smiled at each other as if excited about the next chapter in our lives. We had lived with the constant dread of the next shoe dropping for seven years since Christopher's heart transplant. We felt some real relief to have the ordeal over.

Tom had been wanting to buy a bigger boat for a long time and told me he had found a good one up in Bellingham. He wanted to take me up there to show it to me. I agreed. He had waited a long time for this, and it was time to allow him to realize this dream. I told him we would go check out the boat after the memorial service.

For the next few days until the service, I remember feeling as if I was in the vacuum after a huge explosion. I was exhausted, hollow, and numb but with the sense of impending calamity. When was the numbness going to wear off? It was hot for June. The whole spring had been unseasonably warm. Calls came, people came with food, and flowers started arriving. The obituary was written with great loving care as if it was the most important thing in the world because it was. Christopher's friend Terry came to make picture boards, and we mostly cried but sometimes laughed as we looked at pictures.

The simplest tasks were overwhelming. I wanted to be busy but couldn't muster the energy. I couldn't bear to sit still, couldn't concentrate, couldn't sleep, and couldn't get anything done. It was miserable. I sensed that right around the corner the worst grief of my life was getting ready to attack, and I truly didn't know if I would survive it.

The memorial service was June 19. Pastor David Nelson had grown to love Christopher. "There is nothing we can do or say in the face of death," he said. This was the same way he started every memorial service. "But we can be there."

He told us to share stories as a way to handle our grief. He talked about Christopher and said his name meant "Christ bearer." He talked about how close our church had become due to the focus on this one young life and in support of our family. The pastor read a message I had written on behalf of the family. Here is part of that message:

"We want to thank everyone for coming today to Christopher's celebration of life. For Tom, Jeff, and I, our profound sense of loss is very real, but we also have a profound sense of relief that Christopher is no longer physically and emotionally suffering. We are thankful to the University of Washington Medical Center for the gift of seven additional years of life after the heart transplant. Much of that time was healthy and joyful. However, we are also keenly aware that heart transplants and advanced cancer treatment therapies are a double-edged sword with pain, worry, and much uncertainty for the patient and the family. We are exhausted.

"Christopher fought hard to live this past year, but when the news came the cancer could not be conquered, his exhaustion took over, and he peacefully gave up the fight. He died comfortably and peacefully. Tom, Jeff, and I take great comfort that we were there for Christopher every step of the way. He *never* spent a night alone in the hospital. Due to his intense medical issues, I, as his mother and a nurse, got to spend more time with my twenty-two-year-old son than most mothers get to spend with their sons in entire lifetimes."

When it was time to share stories, Jeff got up to speak:

"I am angry. Angry at the world for stealing my little brother. I am afraid. Afraid that someday I will not be able to remember his face. I am lonely. Lonely because Christopher was my best friend, and I miss him terribly. I am relieved. Relieved his suffering is over, and he has no more pain.

"But above all I am lucky. Lucky to have known him and lucky to have the honor of being his brother. I have never met anyone else like him, and I don't think I ever will.

"There are so many things I could talk about, but I am choosing two—his loyalty and sense of humor.

"Christopher knew many people but only called a few friends. He once told me he was positive each person he called a friend would do anything for him, and after his last few days, I would agree. He absolutely loved his friends, and I know he would do anything for them. During the months in Seattle, before he came back to Olympia, I know it broke his heart he didn't have the energy to phone his friends. I also know he wanted to protect his friends from his pain and bad news.

"When the doctors told us Christopher's treatment had failed, he wrote a list of his friends for me to call. When I returned he looked up with genuine concern in his eyes and asked me, 'How did they take it?' It amazed me that only hours after he learned he was going to die, he was so deeply concerned about how his friends were doing with the news. I would like to thank every one of his friends who came to the hospital or called him during his last days. Thank you for telling the stories you remember of him. You should all know that he knew you were there, and those stories helped him find peace. He loved you all.

"When I hear the word 'strength,' I picture Christopher. He was the strongest person I have ever known. Where others would have become cynical or just plain mean, he didn't. He never complained and never, ever lost his sense of humor.

"I remember a day when he was in Seattle and feeling physically awful from the chemotherapy. He called me and was laughing as he told me about a funny movie he had watched. I came over so we could watch it together, and we ended up laughing until we were crying. Two days before he passed, I was teasing him about a particularly embarrassing story his friends had told me. He opened his eyes, looked at me, laughed, and said, 'Yeah...that was hilarious.'

"The last thing my brother said to me was on the night before he died. It was so fitting that I need to say it, even at the risk of offending some. It was about three in the morning, and his friend Terry and I were up telling stories to him. The nurse had just come in to give him some more pain medication. He knew he was going to be put to sleep by it, and he wanted to let us know. He lifted his head, looked at Terry and me, squeezed my hand, smiled, and said, 'Later, bitches.' That was the last time I saw him conscious and coherent, but I can't imagine a better thing for him to have said. He showed me how valuable a sense of humor is, and we should all try to remember this lesson when we are faced with difficult times and hardships.

"I encourage everyone to remember him happy and healthy. Let's celebrate the time we had with him and have a deeper appreciation for the relationships we still have.

"To grieve for him is healthy and normal, but remember that Christopher would rather have us raise our beers in a toast than hang our heads in sorrow. Thank you."

I still have Jeff's bulletin from the service. On the back of the church program for Christopher's funeral, Jeff wrote, "Christopher, I don't want to be the person sitting here with all eyes watching my tears. I don't want this wrenching in my stomach or this body-shaking emotion that seems on the verge of consuming me at any moment. However, I would endure a thousand lifetimes of this for the memories I have of you. You will always be my brother. Jeff."

It was a very warm June day—over eighty degrees. Over three hundred dressed-up people packed the church. The service was long, and the sanctuary had no air-conditioning. No one left early.

It was as if I viewed the rest of that June through a frosted lens. Images were dull, thoughts were murky and blurred, and actions seemed robotic and surreal. I wanted quiet and peace. I went through the motions of living but as if in slow motion. This fogginess and numbness provided a true survival mechanism because it didn't allow too much grief (or anything else) at any one time.

At times the anger would seethe, and at other times I would have racking sobs. I would hold myself, rock back and forth, and make keening sounds. It was the only thing that would soothe me. At times I could not stand it and would want to get out of my skin. Hard physical work in the garden and long bike rides helped. I was on a roller coaster between recovery meetings with short periods of sobriety and then grief tsunamis numbed with alcohol. I have no memories of Tom and me comforting each other. We just couldn't.

I went to see a woman who had been a coworker for years and who had lost her son to suicide six years before. I knew she had struggled mightily with this loss and now seemed more at peace with it. I wanted to know if she could help me get through this. I knew she had also recently received a diagnosis of breast cancer and was undergoing treatment for it.

I met with her in her office on the seventh floor of the hospital. One whole wall of her office was a huge window overlooking the densely wooded campus of the hospital, and it was a beautiful view on a lovely sunny day. Here was a woman fighting active cancer and surviving her son's suicide, and she was radiating peace and love. She told me there were two things that helped her in the early days. When she was so distraught that no words would come to pray, she would close her eyes and picture herself lying in the hands of God. The second thing she said was she used a prayer she had found in her reading early on after the suicide. It was a slightly modified prayer from the book, *Illuminata; A Return to Prayer*, by Marianne Williamson:

"Dear God, I surrender to you my grief.
I let go all need to struggle.
I relax deeply into things exactly as they are.
I accept life that it might move through me with grace."

She said that when waves of grief felt as if they were going to consume her, she would slowly recite this prayer until she could breathe again.

This prayer repeatedly saved my life. To this day I share it with anyone who is grieving or suffering.

I cannot reconstruct much during the rest of June and early July. I remember long walks in the woods with the dogs, Grace and Bishop, yard work, and many trips to Bellingham to look at the boat, buy the boat, and start cleaning the boat. For the second year, we didn't have our usual family garden, and we used the garden patch as a play area for the dogs. Tom worked furiously on the new boat, which we named the *Christopheles*—a nickname Jeff had given Christopher a few years earlier. It seemed as if Tom thought somehow all the work on this boat was going to bring Christopher back.

Chapter 23

Life Keeps Life-ing

I went back to work in mid-July. My executive assistant, Shannon, made up two sets of stickers. One said, "I'm OK, but please *don't ask* today." The other said, "OK to *ask* today—kind of need to talk about it." I was supposed to wear the sticker that reflected my frame of mind. I don't remember actually ever wearing them, but the thought was so sweet. I know she also ran interference for me and let the staff know how I was doing on any particular day.

At home things were not good between Tom and me. Our home felt very important to me because it held memories of Christopher, but it had the exact opposite effect on Tom. He wanted to be anywhere but home. He talked of wanting to sell the house and get away from the painful memories. I absolutely refused to even consider this. We were grieving totally differently.

I grieved early and openly. I shed lots of tears and needed to talk about Christopher. Tom shut his grief away. He didn't want to talk about it or shed any tears. After about five months, I was starting to come out of the worst of my grieving as Tom was starting to open up the box and let his grief out. He was fairly intolerant of my early grief, and I was no more sympathetic when his began. We had nothing to give each other.

One day we were heading to Bellingham for the boat, and as we drove past the SCCA, I saw tears streaming down Tom's face. I commented that it was good he was finally able to shed some tears. He got uncharacteristically angry with me and told me I had no idea how much pain those tears represented. He wanted to know who I was to tell him that was good. He felt patronized as if I was the grief expert, and I was patting him on the back. There was a chasm developing between us, and I felt a jolt of fear. Maybe we weren't going to make it.

Throughout the fall the daily contact between Tom and me became the cocktail hour when we got home at night. I had gone back to drinking at this point because it seemed the one thing Tom and I shared. During my period of sobriety at the Pete Gross House, Tom had said he was not comfortable with the change in me. "It is like we've been doing the same dance step for thirty years. Now you have changed the step, and I don't know what it is anymore."

We talked about our work situations and nothing else. We shared less and less. I couldn't quite understand why things were so sterile. One day after work, we sat having cocktails, and I addressed this directly. "I don't know what is happening to us, but we are growing miles apart. We have been through too much, and I will be goddamned if we are going to get divorced now!"

I don't remember Tom's reply. There was no intimacy or lovemaking over these six months. There was just pain, and it was not shared pain.

One day in good faith, I was checking Tom's e-mail. We had a social event coming up, and he was the contact. And there it was. "Dear darling" the e-mail began. It went on about how my friend, the nurse practitioner Tom had been consulting about medical questions, couldn't wait to see him the next day for lunch. It talked about how her eyes had met his that night at the church dinner, and her hands had shaken.

I started shaking all over myself. I pushed myself back from the computer and went storming down the hall toward the bedroom. Tom was already in bed. I snapped on the lights. "What the hell did I just read in your e-mail? Oh my God! Are you having an affair?" My head was swirling, and my heart was slamming in my chest. "Darling?" I shrieked. "She calls you *darling*? You have never let me call you one affectionate name in our whole marriage!"

Tom sat up in bed and quietly affirmed my worst fears. He never raised his voice, and he didn't this night either. He gave a weary sigh and told me he was very sorry. It had started out when I had agreed she could be his medical go-to person to answer questions about Christopher's condition so he didn't have to bother me. Tom explained that it had gotten out of hand. It was just emotional and not sexual, but he would tell her the next day it was over.

As my marriage began to crumble, my mom fell ill. On Thanksgiving Day morning (two weeks before I found out about Tom's affair), my mother had called and asked if I could come a little early to help. This was very unusual for my mom. She always had everything handled. When we arrived I couldn't believe my eyes. My mother had aged twenty years in a month. She was ordering my dad around the kitchen (nothing new), but now she was weak and short of breath.

"Mom, what's wrong? Why didn't you tell me sooner you were sick? We didn't have to have Thanksgiving here."

She sheepishly admitted to my sister and me that the past few weeks had been really rough, but she didn't want anyone to worry about her. She took after her own mother and had denial mechanisms that rivaled the best. I knew she was hoping this was nothing and that it would pass. We made Mom and Dad sit down and be the guests as we completed the dinner and cleanup.

Mom promised she would seek medical care and find out what was wrong. She allowed me to make an appointment with a physician I worked with in Centralia who was also a professor at the UW. Mom was losing feeling in her legs and hands. This neuropathy was very unusual as she wasn't diabetic.

About 7:00 a.m. the morning after my sleepless night when I discovered Tom's affair, I got a call from my dad. My mother was in the hospital and having trouble breathing. I headed out to meet them at the hospital, and I called my sister. She was driving the hour south from Seattle. I told her about my discovery of Tom's involvement with one of our closest friends. "That son of a bitch!" she replied. She was both incredulous and seething. I told her we'd better not tell our mother. The last thing she needed was something more to worry about.

My sister and I were again in total shock at how sick our mother was. She was gray and weak and almost too sick to talk. The doctors thought she had an occult cancer. It would explain her symptoms. Her blood oxygen level was horribly low, so she was placed on oxygen. They requested a lung biopsy to see if she had lung cancer.

After the lung biopsy, a very painful procedure, she ended up with a chest tube to keep her lung inflated. She was so uncomfortable she could hardly stand it, and she was in the hospital for over a week. She looked so ill we thought she might die, but she very gradually got better and was discharged home on continuous oxygen. The doctor told her she had pulmonary fibrosis—a condition where the lung tissue hardens, and oxygen does not pass into the blood normally. No one could explain why she had this and also had ascending neuropathy, but the combination had her near death.

The second day of the hospitalization was a Saturday, and Tom wanted to go up with me to see my mom. My poor sister was there and had to act as if nothing had happened. She was about ready to jump out of her skin because she really wanted to kill him. That made two of us! I wasn't just angry, though. I was wounded and humiliated and still so raw from Christopher's death. For months I had wanted love, caring, and intimacy from my husband and had gotten none. I felt forsaken.

There is nothing like infidelity to bring up every single sensitivity, and it did. No one had ever been more horrible to me than myself. If I wasn't accomplishing the miraculous every day, I didn't deserve a place on this Earth. I was a merciless bitch to myself—even though I took great pains to give others breaks. I constantly told my staff not to follow my example at work because I was insane to work so much. They were more mentally and emotionally balanced than I and didn't have to do that to themselves.

Even through the turmoil, there was a part of me deep down that possessed a calm knowing that this was not about me. It was all about Tom and how lost he felt. I had not lost the deep spiritual comfort I had gained at the time of Christopher's death, and I knew I was going to be all right. The more superficial emotions, however, were raw. This included rage. I had never felt such hatred for another person as I felt for that woman. How in the world was I going to avoid her? We saw each other all the time. We were in a tight circle of friends that attended church, boated, and skied together, and it was going to look awfully suspicious if we suddenly weren't all together anymore. Tom had sworn me to secrecy, and I am not sure why I bought into that, but it was my pattern to do as he said.

My mother's illness was all-consuming on the weekends for both my sister and me, and now it became a handy excuse. I begged off the Christmas program where I would have to sing with "that woman," the dinner party before the Christmas concert, and the Friday night get-togethers.

I did go to my pastor. I walked into Pastor David's office and sat down. He said, "So, how is your mom?" He assumed her illness was why I had scheduled a time to see him. I told him how poorly my mother was doing but said that was not why I was there. His eyebrows raised. "What is it?"

All I had to say was, "Tom" and her name ...

He got it. "Oh my!" he said as if someone had just punched him in the stomach. He looked so pained. He knew us all so well and loved us all. He sat there for a long time before he spoke. "How long has it been going on?"

I told him I thought about nine months. Tom had said the affair was over, but if things seemed quite strained, that was why. I had no tears at this point because self-righteous rage filled me.

Our Christmas celebration that year was so awkward and painful. I put Christopher's wooden box of ashes on a small table with a big red Santa hat on top of it. The stocking he had made for our dogs and hamsters when he was about seven hung on the front. Christmas morning Tom, Jeff, and I sat in the living room around our tree with a mountain of presents for Jeff. Jeff and two of his friends had just bought a thirty-foot sailboat, and Tom had gone crazy buying him boat stuff. As Jeff was opening his presents, he joked. "Man, if I had known how many Christmas presents I would have gotten without Christopher, I would have wanted him out of here sooner!"

When presents were opened, we had our first annual Christopher Christmas morning remembrance. Because Christopher loved cigars and Jägermeister, we decided we should smoke cigars and take shots. I wasn't drinking at the time, so I lit up a cigar and smoked as much as I could stand. Tom and Jeff threw back shots of Jäger. The house ended up reeking of cigars for days, and I couldn't get that horrible taste out of my mouth. That was the last annual Christmas remembrance with cigars and Jägermeister. I kept a bottle of that stuff in the freezer for about eight years. It had been Christopher's, and it was hard to let go.

Come January we got back to work and tried to rebuild our marriage. I insisted Tom go to counseling, and he agreed. After only two sessions of joint therapy, it was apparent we had armed our positions and couldn't find any common ground.

We kept trying, though. In late January we decided despite everything to attend a get-together in Vancouver, British Columbia. It included two other couples along with the person with whom Tom had fallen in love and her husband. There she was. Her hair was swept up in a very sensual style, and she was wearing a long, slinky black dress with a slit way up her thigh. She finished off the look with black leather boots.

I wanted to dry up and disappear from the room. I wanted to kill her. I hated myself and the frumpy outfit I had on. I was sure Tom was dying to be with her, and I knew she had dressed that way for my husband—not hers. Her husband looked as if he had swallowed something lethal. His neck was red and blotchy.

How can she dress this way? How can she not be humiliated and ashamed but instead be dressed up as if she is still on the hunt? my mind screamed at me. I had been determined not to drink, but now I set my O'Doule's on the makeshift bar, grabbed a wine glass, and filled it to the brim. I wanted nothing more than to disappear. Instead of speaking my mind and walking out as I should have, I stayed and starting numbing my feelings the only way I knew how—getting drunk.

I knew I was on a path of total annihilation, and I didn't give a shit. In the twelve-step program, I would later learn this behavior is called *drinking at* someone. I was drinking at Tom. Boy, was I going to show him! I eventually had to understand this behavior did nothing to him and only made me want to die from embarrassment—not to mention have a horrible hangover.

I vaguely remember getting back to the hotel and Tom steering me to our room. I was probably staggering drunk by then. I think Tom helped me get my nightgown on and into bed. I believe his plan was to go back to the group for some more partying after I was tucked away. I started sobbing loudly and kept asking him, "Oh my God, why was she dressed like that? Why did you do this? What does she have that I don't have?"

I remember Tom trying to comfort me and telling me to go to sleep—that it would look better in the morning. I passed out, and the room stopped spinning.

The four-hour ride home from Vancouver the next day was horrible. We barely talked, and we each sat in our own misery. My head was in a very toxic place. I felt guilty for leaving my sister alone to take care of my mother. I was angry that the other woman and her husband had shown up at all and angry at myself for gaining weight and getting so drunk the night before. I was angry my son had died and my mom was horribly sick. I was angry I felt behind in my job. I was sure my boss and management team were sick to death of my excuses. Life was horrible. I thought I had paid my dues with Christopher's death, but more bad things could happen. And they did.

In March I found out that the affair had never ended despite assurances. That was the last blow. My passion was gone for anything and anyone. I went through the motions at work, but I had nothing left to give. I had always loved my work, but now it had become a lifeless and exhausting to-do list.

My commute to work took thirty-five minutes, and the CD player was always on *The Power of Now*. It was one of the few times of the day I could stop my fretting, fear, and grief and feel peace in the moment. Tom thought Eckhart Tolle was a joke and dismissed him out of hand. This was just another sign we were on different wavelengths. We had done so well while Christopher was sick. Why couldn't we hold together now he was gone? Jeff later remarked that it was as if Christopher was the rubber band that held us all together, and when the rubber band broke, the pent-up tension from that time blew us all apart.

I decided to resign from my job and announced it at the March department manager's meeting. I am sure some were relieved, but most were very sorry and kind. I felt a burden being lifted. Tom was at a conference in Las Vegas, and when he called to check in, I told him I had resigned. The phone got very quiet. After a pause he asked, "What are you going to do?" This meant, "What about your part of the income?"

"I have no idea, and right now I don't really care," I said quietly. "I will take some time off and then decide."

"You are sure you want to do this?" he asked.

"Extremely sure," I said. I did not want to have to defend myself.

My mom had gone into hospice in late January. My sister and I were there both days every weekend. We bathed and dressed our mother, cleaned the house, cooked the food for the week, paid the bills, did the laundry, and ran any necessary errands. My father was there, and he was doing everything he could for my mom, but he was exhausted. He had lost thirty-five pounds from the constant burden of care. Truly the greatest gift of my mother's illness was the time we spent together. When everyone in my family was well, we were too darned busy "doing" to "be" together.

My mother absolutely adored my children, and she had been the best grandmother to them. She and my dad were always interested in whatever they were doing and came to any and all events. She was a tremendous help during Christopher's heart transplant. His cancer diagnosis seemed too much for her to bear. She was frequently distraught and worried about all of us, and I think it played a big part in her own illness. She could hardly bear it when Christopher died.

Mom was angry about dying. She wasn't ready. She had so much more life she wanted to live. She was only seventy-six. We had always thought she would live into her nineties as her mother had. It was a big blow to see our strong, vibrant mother shrinking and barely able to walk. The pulmonary fibrosis caused great difficulty breathing, and she was on oxygen all the time now. She hated that. The idiopathic neuropathy that had started at her feet had virtually paralyzed her from the waist down. It had also made her hands and arms so weak she could hardly move. Getting her into the car for doctor's appointments was becoming impossible.

One Saturday she said she wanted to tell me something, but she knew I would think she was crazy. I laughed and told her she had been many things over my life, but crazy was never one of them.

"I have seen Christopher," she said. "He has come to see me a couple times."

Tears sprung to my eyes. "Why hasn't he come to see his mother?" I started shaking with emotion.

"I think he is coming to me because he wants to reassure me that dying is going to be OK. That it is very peaceful where he is and to not be afraid," my mother said.

"What does he look like, Mom?" I was now openly crying and wanted to see Christopher with all my heart.

"It looks like him, but he is behind some kind of shimmery screen. He has his baseball cap on and is dressed in a hoodie like always. He is very peaceful, and it gives me a great sense of peace. He keeps saying, 'It's OK, Grandma. It's OK.'"

"It's OK" was a phrase both of us felt Christopher had said to us a few days after the funeral. My mom had called me and said, "Gail, I swear I felt a pat on my arm and heard the words in my head, 'It's OK, Grandma.'"

I about dropped the phone because I had been working out in the yard, and I had felt the very same feeling.

Now we looked at each other with tears in our eyes. "If somebody told me this, I would think they were crazy," Mom finished.

"Remember when Uncle Gene said he saw Jesus as he was waiting to go into surgery?" I asked.

"Yes," Mom said. "I thought he was so sick he was hallucinating. Now I don't know what to think."

I shook my head. "There is so much we don't know. I think the space between life and death might be very thin at times. I totally believe you saw what you saw. If he comes again to see you, would you please tell him to come see me? I miss him terribly."

Then we laughed. We knew this wasn't likely to happen.

My mom had a little inspirational calendar. I looked at March 11, and it said, "God is, and all is well." John Greenleaf Whittier wrote that.

Spiritual strength can come from many sources. It was my sister's birthday, and it was as if God pulled me into his lap that night and said those words while holding me tight. In this transformative moment, peace again flooded my entire being as it had done when I started alcohol recovery the previous March. I was exhausted from lack of sleep and sobbing, but I suddenly felt a peace I hadn't felt about my mom's illness and impending death. I knew once again all was in God's hands and would be OK.

On March 19 Pastor Nordland came to see my mother. He was her favorite. When he and his family had struggled financially as his wife was in school getting her PhD, my mom and dad took them in. They had a tight bond. The pastor pulled his chair right up next to Mom's bed and started talking to her in his large, booming Midwestern accent. She had been deeply comatose for at least three days, but when she heard Pastor Nordland's voice, we could see her eyebrows raise. She was trying to open her eyes.

The Pastor said, "Audrey, don't you know that God is going to take good care of Larry? And don't you know he will also take care of your children?" He then read the Lutheran last rites. Loudly he concluded, "Audrey, I commend your spirit to God."

I realized my mother was no longer moaning with each breath. I looked at my sister. She had noticed the same thing. We stood up and looked at Mom, and she was passing right then. Her breaths went from moans to light breaths to puffs to quiet. Mom had let go and died after Pastor Nordland told her she could and had assured her God would take care of her and all of us. Pastor Nordland was so choked up. He got up quickly and left the room as my sister and I held hands over our mother's body. We were awestruck. Then I said quickly, "Mom, be sure to give Christopher a *big* hug for me."

I spoke at my mom's memorial service, and people commented on how calm and peaceful I seemed. There was a huge amount of peace within me and certainly no fear of death whatsoever. God had once again placed me squarely back into his hands. He helped me then and in the months to come. The words to a favorite hymn by Marty Haugen started showing up out of the blue in my head. "Healer of our every ill, light of each tomorrow, give us peace beyond the pain, and hope beyond our sorrow. You who know our fear and sadness, grace us with your peace and gladness, spirit of all comfort fill our hearts." God was indeed filling my heart, and Christopher was with me each waking moment. I was not alone or afraid.

With mom's death and my preoccupation with her now lifted, I had to, once again, face the issue of my failing marriage. The day after my mom's memorial service Tom and I had a joint counseling session where he admitted he wanted other relationships. I angrily told him to move out. He moved onto the boat on April 1st.

I was finally smart enough to check cell phone records a few weeks later and was shocked to see the extent of their communication for the past many months. I went ballistic and drove like a shot to the boat. I also left a message for his girlfriend and called her an awful name. Did my trusty alcohol have anything to do with my behavior? When I drove home from yelling at Tom, I could easily have been cited for a DUI. I couldn't have cared less, though. I actually thought if I got a DUI, it might stop my drinking. This is how warped my thinking had become about my alcohol use.

At long last I was too angry, humiliated, and broken to put up a good front. I called Jeff. "Jeff," I told our son, "your dad has been having an affair since sometime last year. This is why the marriage has been in such trouble. I have known since last December, but your father swore me to silence. I can't pretend anymore."

There was silence on the phone for several moments. "I will be there in a little while," Jeff said quietly.

It was a workday when we talked. I don't know what excuse he made, but he arrived from Seattle a couple hours later. He was so angry at his father. Jeff had called his dad on the way home, and the conversation hadn't gone well.

After we talked for a while, Jeff went outside, took an ax, and spent hours cutting down a large tree. When he got done, his hands were a mess of broken blisters, and he was exhausted. "I had to get that energy out somehow, Mom," he said. "Sorry about the tree, but I feel like killing Dad. Cutting down a tree was a better alternative."

He stayed with me until after dinner, and then he headed back up to Seattle. The next morning I awoke to Tom walking into the bedroom. He sat on the bed and very quietly said, "I thought we were going to keep Jeff out of this."

I was done defending myself. "This is your dirty little secret, and I have been stupid enough to keep it for you. I am done with that. From now on it is all out in the open."

I was really on my own now for the first time in my life. My heart still ached with the loss of Christopher and my mom—even though I knew spiritually they were both with me. I knew I had to take care of myself. I restarted the home remodel Tom and I had begun that Christopher's cancer had cut short. Shannon, truly my angel through all this, had the wonderful idea of a work party to paint the inside of my house. One of my friends from the hospital, Delynn, had a great eye for color, so she came up, and we picked paint for the family room, living and dining room, hallway, and master bedroom. The walls had always been white, and it was now time for some color. April 30 came, and a dozen former coworkers showed up in work clothes and started painting like crazy. By the end of the day, nearly every room in the house was painted in warm and beautiful colors. It looked like *my* new home, and it lifted my spirits so to have these people spend their entire Saturday helping me out.

Now off work for a few months, I developed a pattern of getting up in the morning to take my two black Labs for a one-hour walk in the woods. Then I came home to work all day inside and outside the house. I took out all the kitchen cabinets and the sink myself, ripped out all the carpeting, replaced all the exterior light fixtures, hung curtains and blinds, and picked out new cabinets, carpeting, and wood flooring. It was a cathartic process. I was ripping out the old and making the house my own. I had never had the confidence to do any remodeling or even pick paint colors. I was always led to believe by Tom that I was totally incompetent in all those areas. As the house came together, it looked better and better. I felt both vindicated and validated. The labor was physically demanding, but that work, long daily walks, fresh air, lack of stress from an overwhelming career, and the spiritual gift given to me those months before Christopher's death left me with a quiet mind and serenity. I still, however, could not quit drinking.

Mid-May I went to Las Vegas with my dad and brother-in-law for a three-day trip. Dad needed a getaway, liked playing blackjack, and invited me to come along. It was all very nice, but on our day to return home, Dad and Uncle Tom got on an earlier flight. I decided to have a glass of wine at the airport around noon. That glass led to a return to the casinos and ten hours of drinking wine by myself. I blacked out at the Venetian and came to waiting for my plane to take off at 10:00 p.m. Thank God I had my purse, wallet, and all my credit cards. I had blacked out many times in my life but never by myself in a distant city. The plane ride home was nauseating and rough.

The next day I do not ever want to relive. All the pain of Christopher's death, the agony of the affair, the broken marriage, and my mother's death hit at once. With the self-loathing of my alcoholism and a hangover, I wanted to die. I remember sitting on the top step of my front porch sobbing and rocking back and forth with Christopher's picture clutched to my chest. That was my lowest point. It was May 13, 2005—one month to the day before the first anniversary of Christopher's death—and I was done. I was now willing to do anything to relieve my alcoholic obsession.

I started going to meetings every day and reconnected with my sponsor. Five days later I went to an alcohol assessment appointment. The counselor asked me many questions about my drinking, and at the end confirmed what I already knew without question. I was an alcoholic.

I started attending a daily 5:15 p.m. meeting called "Happy Hour." It was the perfect time of day. I could finish my remodeling work, clean up, and get myself out of the house. It was the same time of day I would have started drinking. This meeting helped me find serenity each day, and my craving for alcohol subsided once again—this time for good.

On June 13 (the first anniversary of Christopher's death) Jeff wanted to be home for a quiet reflective day. As it turned out, it was the day the final touches of all the remodeling came together. The carpet was installed, all the windows were replaced and cleaned, the kitchen countertops were on, the kitchen sink went in, the last of the laminate floor was finished, and the furniture went back into place.

The house was peaceful, calm, and very beautiful. It felt like mine. I felt a deep serenity and gratitude for my home, my sobriety, and my living son who was there with me. I felt as if Christopher knew a new life would begin for me, and he wanted the high point to be on the anniversary of his death. I felt he was saying to me, "See, Mom? You can do this."

A month later I went back to work as the nurse manager of the emergency room at Providence Centralia Hospital. Christopher and I had spent countless hours in emergency rooms over the preceding eight years, and I had the greatest admiration for the physicians and staff who worked in ERs. If I could do anything to make their lives even a bit easier, I wanted to try. There were terrible morale issues in the ER, a computerized medical record installation had failed during the summer, and a huge construction project to build a completely new emergency department was beginning.

My marriage was not over yet. We tried to reconcile one more time six months later, but there was nothing left to rebuild. Jeffrey's metaphor later was, "Mom and Dad chopped down the tree of their marriage to fuel the fire of support needed for Christopher."

That was how it felt, and I knew we were done. The marriage dissolution was final September 5, 2006. I was standing on my own two feet. The job was good, my passion for work had returned, and I was happily absorbed. I was sober and totally committed to working a twelve-step program. There was so much to be grateful for.

The spiritual journey that began three months before Christopher's death continued in earnest. It had a life of its own. I never quit going to my wonderful church, but vast horizons now opened up through people, books, and CDs that came into my life at just the right time. In and around the grief were prolonged periods of joy and peace I never knew existed. I knew that alcohol was numbing all my fears but didn't realize that it was also taking away happiness and joy. All fear of financial insecurity as a single person left me. Life took on a flow and ease. I became increasingly content. This two-year process carried me out of a thirty-one-year marriage that I left kicking and screaming and into a new life of hope and joy. It also led me into a wonderfully fun and loving second marriage.

I have a vivid image of going to the Puyallup Fair that September of 2006. It was a beautifully warm sunny day. I had a cute new Honda Civic that I had bought with my own money, a CD playing loudly (Tom hated loud music), and the windows all rolled down (Tom hated the windows rolled down). I was going to see the dahlias, eat scones, and enjoy a chocolate-dipped ice cream cone with nuts. I had lost seventeen pounds from the "divorce diet" and felt free and invincible. I had just walked out of my newly painted, newly remodeled home. It was truly *my* home, and I was on top of the world. Not every day was so grand as this one, but more and more I felt as if I was coming into my own. My opinion mattered, I felt attractive, I was financially independent, and I had a whole new chapter of life ahead of me.

Life, I thought, *might keep on life-ing for quite a while!*

Chapter 24

The Last and Best Lesson

Christopher's writing here describes the peace he found while waiting for a heart, but I believe it also describes the peace he found again when he knew he had lost his fight with cancer. I end this book with his words.

I believe all people for a short while reach the pinnacles of their existences. For each person it comes at a different time. It could be at birth or right before death, but all at once the muddled uncertainties and false things of importance congeal and in that moment of clarity, everything falls away. Everything that has always seemed most important is seen for what it is — useless, irrelevant baggage crowding life.

For better or worse, I have already experienced my pinnacle. It happened two years ago in May. I was very sick with heart failure and in the ICU at the University of Washington Hospital. One day I was put on the priority one heart transplant list for all the Western states. Being the stubborn, arrogant person I am, I probably have a stronger denial mechanism than most. My castle of defense held up against the siege of empirical evidence for an admirably long time. The broken record playing in my head was repeating,

"There is no way you are going to let this thing beat you!" Unfortunately, for the first time in my life, I was completely helpless to change my horrible position even in the slightest. However, I wouldn't allow myself to believe this for many days.

No matter how strong I could try to be, my ramparts were bound to fall. All at once hope, strength, and resolve were sucked out of my life like so many dust bunnies, and I was left in a vacuum. I began a mental and emotional free fall down the pit of despair without the slightest splinter of hope to grasp for. The pain that tore my soul to little pieces could not be inflicted in the physical realm.

Over the following days, I experienced the worst period of my life—a time when life held no meaning for me. I was certain death wouldn't be entirely a bad thing, and life was only a fraction of a point better. I look back now, and I am very scared of what I might have done if I had had the means to end my life at that point. The depression was so deep that even nothing meant nothing.

The only way I could even sort of cope with the pain was to accept death for all it was. The end. It was during this process I lost my belief in the Christian religion. Have you ever had to accept your own death? Not just consider it but surrender to it? Believe it or not, it was easier to know I was going to die rather than try to regain my resolve. That was impossible.

I began to live my life for every second rather than every day because of how finite I saw the remainder of my existence. During this two-week period, I reached what I consider as close to perfection as I am capable of. All trappings fell away, and I saw what was really important in my life—family. The ones I loved unconditionally who loved me unconditionally back.

During that period I came to enjoy my father, mother, and brother like never before. Realizing my time was short, every second I spent with them was a gift. In a situation as grave as mine, I decided to make every moment quality time. I had always been very close to my mother, but my father and brother had been close yet somehow distant. In those days it seems we laughed harder than ever before, and we cried out more pain than I ever thought possible. Every blink of an eye and every syllable carried more weight than the sum of all my actions in recent memory.

For the only time in my life, my purpose was as clear as it could ever be. I had to put aside all petty differences and arguments I had ever had with any of them and love them as hard and as much as I could with the time I had left. They felt the same, and our family melded into something I never considered possible—a single entity with one purpose: to love and support one another. In this overwhelming love, I came to feel, for lack of better words, a complete peace.

I felt that as long as I had these three people to love me, nothing else mattered—not a severely handicapped life and not even death. I wish there was a way I could describe the magnitude of these events better, but I cannot paint my feelings and memories.

On the fateful night of May 30, I found out there was a heart for me. I found out the chances of my perishing were greatly reduced, and I faced it with a confident indifference. I could have died during that period, but I wasn't afraid of that eventuality. I knew what life was all about. Those I loved most in the world surrounded me, and I had made my peace with this flawed existence. I was ready.

Painkillers and Gummi Bears

If it seems as though I cherish the worst experience in my life, it is because I do. I don't cherish all the pain and suffering of my physical body, but I certainly cherish the singular clarity upon which I could focus the sum of all I am and all I ever will be—love. My family is undoubtedly the most important thing in my life, and it always will be.

Epilogue

Four years before Christopher's death, Jeff and two of his buddies started talking about sailing around the world. We didn't take it too seriously. However, the guys had a five-year plan. They figured they each had to save sixty thousand dollars...and learn how to sail. The three of them bought a thirty-foot sailboat and started taking sailing courses. Then they got serious and bought a well-seasoned oceangoing forty-four-foot boat recently vacated by a family who had circumnavigated the globe.

A little over a year after Christopher died, Jeff, Matt, and Casey quit their high-paying engineering jobs and set sail from Seattle. Pastor David blessed the boat in a little ceremony as part of a bigger send-off celebration. They returned in September 2007 after circumnavigating the world. They posted over ten thousand pictures and hundreds of posts. Googling "Adventures of the *Sohcahtoa*" will yield their old website and blog with many photos.

Christopher's death made final Jeff's decision to go on the trip. He realized how unpredictable and short life could be. Jeff took a small box of Christopher's ashes and sprinkled them throughout his trip at memorable spots or on memorable days. Jeff says now he isn't sure if his underlying reason for the trip wasn't just to get away and escape his problems. Leaving everything familiar and isolating himself on a sailboat with only his thoughts and two other people turned into a grisly way of coping with his losses. Many times were very painful and lonely.

He grappled with four big things on the boat trip: fear of dying at sea, grief at the loss of his brother, missing Christina terribly, and anger at his father over the infidelity. Jeff realized as the boat started heading back home (it is one big circle, after all!) that he had all sorts of unresolved grief and anger at the breakup of his parents' marriage. He was still livid at his dad.

A huge favor Tom did for Jeff and the crew started thawing the relationship. At one point they ended up stranded on the small island of Bonaire off the coast of Venezuela. A crucial piece of equipment had broken, and Jeff was having little luck obtaining a replacement. On May 22, 2007, four months before the journey was complete, Tom spent twenty-three hours on three flights with over ninety pounds of boat hardware flying to Bonaire to help the crew of the *Sohcahtoa* fix their problem. Tom was not a comfortable international traveler, so the trip took a lot of effort and adrenaline.

As the boat got fixed, Tom and the crew spent four days diving in the most incredibly clear and beautiful surroundings. The last night before Tom flew home, many drinks were knocked back, and two years of venom came spewing out of Jeff all over Tom.

Jeff sent me an e-mail the next day. "Seeing Dad opened up a whole big can of turmoil in me, and I did what I seem to do best when I feel trapped by my emotions—I got really drunk. I thought I was further along with my grief than I really am. I just couldn't handle it. I also realized how incredibly lonely I am on this boat. I am finishing this trip, but it is no longer a place I want to be.

"I have been harboring a resentment of Dad for a long time. I think it has been partially for your sake, partially for Christopher's sake, and mostly for mine. The parts for you and Christopher have mainly been what has kept me in this kind of stasis where I choose not to resolve my issues. I have been feeling kind of like the champion against Dad because it is pretty obvious I am the only one who can really hurt him. I have kept it up longer than I should. It has been over two years since I chopped down the tree at our house. I have to get rid of this resentment because I think it is what is creating a big emotional logjam and preventing me from dealing with other things such as Christopher's and Grandma Audrey's deaths.

"I know it is going to be tough for both of us, but I really need to stop taking your side on this. It can't be 'Mom and Jeff' against Dad.

My future road is going to suck. It means I am going to have to forgive Dad and accept Dad's new relationship. I can't stay in this boiling sea of emotional turmoil that lies just under the surface just because I think Dad deserves to suffer. That isn't me. When did I start enjoying knowing someone is suffering because of my intolerance or lack of acceptance? That is something ugly I don't want as part of me. I must open that door and let light into those dark places I never go but affect me in all sorts of ways. Long story short, I am going to work to forgive Dad. I am also going to have to work on this guilt for the hurt I have caused him, so maybe I am going to have to forgive myself as well."

It has taken time, but today Jeff and Tom are again quite close—as it should be.

When Jeff got back to Seattle and returned to Christina, he knew he had found his new home. She was the bedrock he needed as he rebuilt his life, and he has done that with her help. Pastor David Nelson married them January 3, 2009. They are now the parents of Trevor Christopher Stewart, my darling three-year-old grandson. Trevor's due date was calculated per standard procedure from the probable date of conception—June 13—the same day as Christopher's death. The universe works in miraculous ways.

Today Jeff feels he has worked through the pressure he felt in high school and college to be pulled into a role or to be a person he "should" be. He is much more of an introvert, and if he is uncomfortable in a social situation, he just leaves or doesn't feel forced to talk or entertain.

"I don't have to fit in or participate. I can just be quiet," he recently told me. "I feel much more peaceful these days. I enjoy small groups and a few close friends and mostly family."

When Tom moved out in April 2005, he lived on the forty-five foot boat we bought right after Christopher's death—the *Christopheles*. He was there for over a year. He continued counseling and started to find his footing. He realized he'd lived his entire life as he "should." He had been a good son, good student, Eagle Scout, good provider, businessperson, and family man. Now he started living life the way he wanted. He paid a very high price for his new beginning. He left our church and all our close friends. He called himself "the pariah." He went through his own hell. About a year after our divorce in September 2006, he moved in with his girlfriend. They married in February 2008. They are very happy and continue to pursue boating together with a passion. They see Jeff and his family often.

Today Jeff understands that both his parents are happier with their new spouses. "You both laugh a lot more!" he told me recently. He still regrets not being able to "go home" and be together with his family, but we all miss that. Some days the urge to be back together as a complete family overwhelms us all. Jeff loves his stepfather and stepmother, but it is not the same as having his mom and dad together in the house where he was raised. And of course, Christopher is missing.

As for me, I feel lucky to have had the time I had with Christopher. As I said at his memorial service, due to his illness, I got to spend more time with my son in his twenty-two years than most mothers get to spend with their sons in entire lifetimes. The serenity I found during the terrible time when Christopher was leaving us is still with me. It has faded some over the years, but my crazy workaholic tendencies and the screaming demons—the chattering committee in my head—are diminished greatly. My spiritual journey has become a way of life.

The one great outcome of my successful workaholic career is that I was able to retire at fifty-six. Jeff and I joke that this trait he hated in me has now allowed me to be "Grandma Gail" and totally available to Jeff and his family. I am following a tradition my own grandmother set when she came to our house weekly to do our washing and care for her grandchildren. Today I remind Jeff of his beloved great-grandmother and of my mom, his Grandma Audrey, by taking care of his son, doing his laundry, and cooking for his freezer. Beyond the family I am blessed to be the coordinator of a large community garden through my church that grows crops for our local food bank. I also have the privilege of helping other women find and maintain sobriety. Today I am so grateful for my peace of mind and a life of service.

A month after my divorce was final, I invited a man out to coffee. (It was very forward of me!) We knew each other casually from a Sunday night twelve-step meeting I had attended for a year. His name was Tom too, and he had twenty years of sobriety. Dating scared me. I had married my high school sweetheart, and we had been together for thirty-six years. It turned out God had a plan, though, and I never had to date another man. The wonderful new Tom and I fell in love and married in September 2008.

My new Tom is just like me, and thanks to our sobriety and the twelve-step work we each have done, we love ourselves—the good and the bad—so we can love each other fiercely, which we do. I wanted my first husband to fix me with his strength and integrity. Today I know I am far from perfect, but I don't need any fixing.

The years between 1997 and 2006 were ones I didn't think I could live through. A good friend recently described grief as something that starts out as 100 percent and over time diminishes but never goes away. I understand that. The cloud of 100 percent grief has slowly decreased over the years to maybe 5 to 10 percent today. Most of my days, I can think of my son, smile, and silently say, "Hi, honey." Occasionally I find myself weepy and morose as if Christopher's death occurred yesterday. That is how grief is. It can come in like a wave. Even though I love my marriage today, at times I think back to our family, and the longing to be back there nearly strangles me.

Did I want my son to die? Never. Did I want my thirty-one-year marriage to end? No. Did I want to admit my alcoholism? Not at all. Did I have to accept all these things kicking and screaming? Yes, I did. Were there times I screamed at God and wanted to die? Yes, there were. All these events, however, fundamentally changed me. They allowed me to drop who I thought I had to be and allowed me to just *be*. Eckhart Tolle says we never know what is good or bad for us. I can agree with that today.

I would give anything to have my son back, but I rest in the knowledge he was truly at peace when he died. If Christopher had died afraid or angry, I think my heart would still be broken in a much worse way. I sensed his peace, and I carry him in my heart. His picture is my computer screen saver, so daily I can say, "Hi, sweetheart. I love you."

I have asked him for help many times during the writing of this book, and I feel I have received it. I know that someday, somehow, we will see each other again, and it will be a most wondrous and happy reunion.

I can't wait.

Acknowledgments

First and foremost I thank my sister, Christopher's and Jeff's Auntie Chris. Without her I would have never been able to get through then or now. Your presence in the events of this book was so much bigger than I was able to portray. Take good care of yourself. I want us to live to be very old together!

Eternal thanks to Pastor David I. Nelson and his wife, Mary, whose friendship, wisdom, and loving support throughout the seven years of Christopher's illnesses were invaluable. For everything from your special present to Christopher to your impeccable timing of showing up minutes before each "bad news" episode, I thank you. As you always say, "Grace, peace, and all that good stuff to you."

Thanks to Shannon Akin, my executive assistant from 1997–2004. You came into my life five months before the cardiac crisis and stayed at my side through it all. God sent you to me as my personal angel, and I don't know how I would have survived without your beautifully homemade cards, daily talks, and Friday lunches.

Thanks to Lester Krupp, Christopher's English teacher at Yelm High School, who inspired and prodded Christopher to write his journal. Much of that journal appears in this book. Being able to write about his illness was so important to Christopher, and now those words mean so much to me. I doubt Christopher would have undertaken this writing without your encouragement.

Thanks to the University of Washington Heart Transplant Program for saving Christopher's life in 1997. Daniel Fishbein, MD, was outstanding in the critical period and during the first few years. Kevin O'Brien, MD, who managed Christopher's care during the maintenance phase, was as well. I thank RN and heart transplant coordinator Vic Himes for her outstanding outpatient management. She and RN Sandy Cruse worked with the transplant cardiologists and were a wealth of information. Vic, you will forever hold such a special place in my heart for your help. You had a great way of working with Christopher. You knew when to joke and be like "one of the guys" and when to really show how much you cared.

Thanks to a particularly excellent and compassionate nurse, Rhoni Gendron, who cared for Christopher during the six weeks he was at UW Hospital for the heart transplant.

Thanks to the Olympia physicians for all their help over the seven years. Special thanks to Chris Griffith, MD, Mike Matlock, MD, Bill Mitchell, MD, and Bill Brennan, MD. You all are the best at what you do.

The Seattle Cancer Care Alliance and the Pete Gross House were our homes for three months, and we were grateful to be able to access a world-renowned center for Christopher's care. Dorothy Ghaly, RN, and Mark Matsui, PA, were particularly wonderful to Christopher at the SCCA. Eddie Dickerson was the angel that drove the SCCA shuttle with love every day. Thank you.

Thanks to all the friends at St. Mark Lutheran Church who prayed for us, kept us supplied with what Jeff called "Lutheran casseroles," performed a home remodel, and were there for us after it was all over.

Thanks to my former husband, my "first" Tom, who was always there for the family. Thanks also for proofreading the book and calling it a "balanced accounting."

Special thanks to my Spiritwind friends—Ron and Judy Wilson, Dick and Trudy Olson, and Stan and Dalene Feero. Singing together from 1997–2005 was a special spiritual gift that helped so much. Also thanks to Lloyd and Barb Schneider. You are dear and helpful friends.

Thanks to my Providence Centralia management team and staff. You supported me and did your jobs even when I was in crisis. It was a privilege to work with you all. Thanks to all my St. Peter Hospital work friends of twenty-five years who donated sick leave for me and supported me emotionally. Thanks to my wonderful bosses at Providence, Dave Bjornson, Scott Bond, and Steve Burdick. You gave me the leave I needed to attend to my family.

Thanks to Christopher's good buddies—especially Terry, Tyler, Jessie, Talus, Brad, Robert, Alex, Zak, and Za. You were always there for him, and he was there for you. That is what true friendship is all about.

Thanks to my sponsor, Gracie, and to all my recovery friends who supported me in the early days after Christopher's death and still do into my ninth year of sobriety. I would not have survived without you all, the twelve-step program, and my Higher Power.

I thank so many family members, on both sides, and friends for their support of all kinds and for helping us pay our rent at the Pete Gross House in Seattle. Special thanks to Betty Rose who contributed the equivalent of a king's ransom to help us.

I do not know how to repay my editor, Cathy Short, who agreed to do this as a volunteer project. If I had known how much work this was going to be for her, I never would have had the guts to ask! A million thanks for helping me shape Christopher's writing and my own into a coherent book. Together, Cathy and I thank the many readers of the draft manuscript for their valuable comments.

Thank you to my wonderful son, Jeff, and his blessing of a wife, Christina, for allowing me to be such a part of your lives. Jeff has supported the book idea from the start and contributed the clever chapter titles, and much content.   Thank you for my grandson Trevor Christopher, and for the next grandchild due in June of 2015.

Last but absolutely not least, thank you to my wonderful husband, my "New Tom." You gave me the gift of early retirement so I could have time and energy to work on this project. You are my big, handsome, sexy goofball and I love you with all my heart. I cannot believe how very blessed I am. As you always say, "I've never had it so good!"

Made in the USA
San Bernardino, CA
11 February 2015